SECOND EDITION

TOP NOTCH 3

Copy & Go

Ready-Made Interactive Activities for Busy Teachers

Joan Saslow • Allen Ascher

With Wendy Pratt Long

PEARSON
Longman

Top Notch: English for Today's World 3, Second Edition
Copy & Go: Ready-made Interactive Activities for Busy Teachers

Copyright © 2011 by Pearson Education, Inc.
All rights reserved.

No part of this publication may be reproduced,
stored in a retrieval system, or transmitted
in any form or by any means, electronic, mechanical,
photocopying, recording, or otherwise,
without the prior permission of the publisher.

Pearson Education, 10 Bank Street, White Plains, NY 10606

Staff credits: The people who made up the *Top Notch Copy & Go 3*, **Second Edition** team, representing editorial, production, design, and manufacturing are: Rhea Banker, Elizabeth Carlson, Mindy DePalma, Dave Dickey, Aliza Greenblatt, Gosia Jaros-White, Mike Kemper, Barbara Sabella, and Nicole Santos.

Cover Design: Rhea Banker
Cover Photograph: Sprint/Corbis
Text composition: Quarasan
Text font: ITC Stone Sans 10.5/12.5

Photo credits: Page 13 (x-ray) Maxine Hall/Corbis, (checkup) Shutterstock.com, (shot) Shutterstock.com; p. 47 (top left) Jose Luis Pelaez, Inc./Corbis, (top right) James P. Blair/Corbis, (bottom left) Thinkstock, (bottom right) Jim Arbogast/Getty Images.

Illustration credits: Stephen Attoe: pages 53, 67, 77, 79; Deborah Crowle: page 75; Leanne Franson: page 25; Brian Hughes: pages 67, 77; Suzanne Mogensen: page 25; Dusan Petriçic: pages 13, 63; Gail Piazza: page 13

ISBN-13: 978-0-13-247070-4
ISBN-10: 0-13-247070-5

PEARSON LONGMAN ON THE WEB

Pearsonlongman.com offers online resources for teachers and students. Access our Companion Websites, our online catalog, and our local offices around the world.

Visit us at **www.pearsonlongman.com**.

Printed in the United States of America
2 3 4 5 6 7 8 9 10–V042–15 14 13 12 11

INTRODUCTION

Copy & Go 3 Second Edition gives students additional practice with the vocabulary, grammatical structures, and social language presented in the Second Edition of *Top Notch 3* Student's Book. With an emphasis on goal-oriented language usage, *Copy & Go 3* Second Edition is intended to provide students with extensive speaking practice that is useful, interesting, and above all, fun.

Copy & Go 3 Second Edition consists of two parts. The first part contains 40 reproducible classroom activities—four per unit (one per lesson)—each taking between 20 and 30 minutes of classroom time. These include role plays, information-gap activities, board games, card games, and charades—all designed to get students to interact in pairs and small groups with minimal teacher input. The task-oriented nature of the activities encourages students to recycle vocabulary from the units, to practice the grammatical structures, and to use the social language in an unself-conscious manner, combining the elements of production and practice seamlessly and painlessly. A lesson plan for each activity is provided.

While it is possible for teachers to pick and choose these activities for use as a post-unit review, it is recommended that teachers use the activities as an immediate reinforcement following each lesson.

LESSON PLAN

The lesson plan that accompanies each reproducible activity provides the following information:

- **Activity Type**—the type of exercise; for example, board game
- **Target Language**—the specific vocabulary, grammatical structures, and social language being covered; for example, information questions
- **Materials**—notes for preparation of the worksheets as well as other supplies needed; for example, dice, coins, markers, and pencils
- **Preparation**—suggestions for a presentation of the target structures and background information that students will need in order to carry out the activity
- **Procedure**—step-by-step instructions for carrying out the activity
- **Options/Alternatives**—alternative methods of performing the activity (for example, different group sizes, faster/slower options), as well as possible extensions of the activity
- **Answer Key**—where applicable

The second part contains ten "Find Someone Who . . ." activities that correspond to the ten units in the Student's Book. They are designed to get your students to stand up and mingle in order to talk with and get specific information from each other. Instructions on how to use these "stand-up" activities can be found on page 82.

CONTENTS

Unit : Lesson	Activity Type	Target Language
1 : 1	❶ Information gap	Tag questions
1 : 2	❷ Card game	The past perfect
1 : 3	❸ Trivia game	Being culturally literate Manners and etiquette vocabulary
1 : 4	❹ Survey Discussion	Discussing how culture changes over time
2 : 1	❺ Charades	Must
2 : 2	❻ Bingo game	Symptoms vocabulary Medical procedures vocabulary
2 : 3	❼ Concentration	Types of medical treatments
2 : 4	❽ Conversation	Making an appointment Describing symptoms at a doctor's office
3 : 1	❾ Sentence-creation card game	Causatives get, have, and make Some ways to help out another person
3 : 2	❿ Information gap	The passive causative
3 : 3	⓫ Card game	Evaluating the quality of service
3 : 4	⓬ Bingo game	Planning an event
4 : 1	⓭ Guessing game	Noun clauses
4 : 2	⓮ Questions and answers	Noun clauses: embedded questions
4 : 3	⓯ Find someone who . . .	Describing reading habits Some ways to enjoy reading vocabulary
4 : 4	⓰ Reading materials game	Types of reading materials Discussing the quality of reading materials
5 : 1	⓱ Charades	Indirect speech: imperatives
5 : 2	⓲ Board game	Indirect speech: say and tell Tense changes
5 : 3	⓳ Bingo game	Severe weather and other natural disasters vocabulary Adjectives of severity
5 : 4	⓴ Discussion	Emergency preparations and supplies

Unit : Lesson	Activity Type	Target Language
6 : 1	㉑ Sentence-creation card game	Was / were going to
6 : 2	㉒ Role play	Perfect modals
6 : 3	㉓ Find someone who …	Discussing skills, abilities, and qualifications
6 : 4	㉔ Concentration game	Discussing factors that promote success
7 : 1	㉕ Sentence-completion game	Ways to commemorate a holiday Adjective clauses
7 : 2	㉖ Board game	Adjective clauses with subject and object relative pronouns
7 : 3	㉗ Questions game	Exchanging information about holidays
7 : 4	㉘ Trivia game	Getting married vocabulary Ways to commemorate a holiday vocabulary
8 : 1	㉙ Sentence-construction game	Conditional sentences
8 : 2	㉚ Conversation	Taking responsibility for a mistake The past unreal conditional
8 : 3	㉛ Card game	Descriptive adjectives
8 : 4	㉜ Card game	Discussing the impact of inventions / discoveries
9 : 1	㉝ Board game	Non-count nouns that represent abstract ideas
9 : 2	㉞ Concentration	Political terminology vocabulary Political and social beliefs vocabulary Some controversial issues vocabulary
9 : 3	㉟ Information-gap crossword puzzle	Unit 9 social language, vocabulary, grammar
9 : 4	㊱ Discussion	Discussing controversial issues politely Debating the pros and cons of issues
10 : 1	㊲ 20 questions	Prepositions of geographical place
10 : 2	㊳ Board game	Too + adjective and infinitive
10 : 3	㊴ Bingo game	Warning about possible risks Describing the natural world vocabulary
10 : 4	㊵ Question and answer game	Describing the natural world vocabulary Discussing solutions to global warming

"Find Someone Who . . ." Activities . . . . page 82

Activity 1 — PAIR WORK – Information gap

Unit 1 – Lesson 1

Target Language	Materials
Tag questions	One copy of the worksheet cut in half for each pair of students, pens or pencils

PREPARATION (5 minutes)

- Write on the board a few sentences about yourself, using a variety of tenses. Some sentences should be true, and some should be false. For example:
  I was born in Canada.
  I didn't grow up in Hong Kong.
  I'm an architect.
  I'm going to fly to Munich tonight.

- Call on students to confirm each statement by asking you a tag question. Remind them to form their questions based on whether or not they think the information is true. (*You were born in Canada, weren't you? You didn't grow up in Hong Kong, did you? You're not an architect, are you?* etc.)

- Answer the questions with short answers.

PROCEDURE (10–15 minutes)

- Divide students into pairs. Distribute half a worksheet to each student.

- Give students a few minutes to complete the first column of the worksheets. They should use true information for some sentences, and they should use false information for some. Make sure students fill in only the first column at this point.

- Explain the activity: Partners switch worksheets. Student A reads the first sentence on Student B's worksheet. He or she asks a tag question to confirm the information. He or she should form the question based on what he or she expects the answer to be.

- For example, if Student B wrote *I was born in Vietnam*, but Student A thinks the sentence is false, then he or she asks *You weren't born in Vietnam, were you?* If Student A thinks the sentence is true, then he or she asks *You were born in Vietnam, weren't you?*

- Based on Student B's answer, Student A then marks the original sentence *True* or *False*. If the sentence is false, then he or she asks about and notes the correct information on the worksheet.

- Students continue as above, taking turns asking about each sentence, until both students have asked questions about all of their partner's information.

OPTIONS/ALTERNATIVES (5 minutes)

- Invite students to share with the class information they learned about their partners.

2 ■ LESSON PLAN

Student A's Sentences	True or False? (Student B to fill in.)	True Information (Student B to fill in if Student A's sentence is false.)
I was born in _____.	T F	
I grew up in _____.	T F	
I can _____.	T F	
I've never been to _____.	T F	
Tonight I'm going to _____.	T F	
I like _____ a lot.	T F	
I am _____.	T F	
I don't usually _____.	T F	

-------- ✂ ---

Student B's Sentences	True or False? (Student A to fill in.)	True Information (Student A to fill in if Student B's sentence is false.)
I was born in _____.	T F	
I grew up in _____.	T F	
I can _____.	T F	
I've never been to _____.	T F	
Tonight I'm going to _____.	T F	
I like _____ a lot.	T F	
I am _____.	T F	
I don't usually _____.	T F	

PHOTOCOPIABLE   COPY & GO 3 ■ ACTIVITY 1

Activity 2 — GROUP WORK – Card game

Unit 1 – Lesson 2

Target Language	Materials
The past perfect	Each group needs one copy of the worksheet cut into cards, scrap paper for keeping score, pens or pencils

PREPARATION (5 minutes)

- Write the following two sentences on the board:
  When Harry went to Rome, he had already started his Italian class.
  When Harry started his Italian class, he had already gone to Rome.

- Call on a student to explain the difference between the two sentences. (In the first sentence, Harry started his Italian class, then he went to Rome. In the second, Harry went to Rome, then he started his Italian class.)

PROCEDURE (15 minutes)

- Have students form groups of two, three, or four. One player in each group mixes up the cards and places them facedown in a pile.

- Explain the game: The first player takes a card and reads the two sentences aloud. He or she makes one sentence in the past perfect with the information on the card. Encourage students to use time expressions, such as *before, after, yet, already, by the time,* etc. **Note:** the sentence must be correct in grammar as well as meaning.

- If the sentence is correct, the player gets one point. He or she then may take the one point and end his or her turn. Or, the player may take another card and make another sentence for the opportunity to get one more point. If the player makes a correct sentence, he or she then gets two points. If the sentence is incorrect, the player gets zero points for that turn.

- The student must decide if he or she will take another turn before taking the next card.

- Any time a player doesn't make a correct sentence, his or her turn is over and he or she receives no points.

- If a student draws a *Lose a turn* card, his or her turn is immediately over.

- On any one turn, each player must turn over at least one card, but not more than three.

- Play continues until there are no more cards. The player with the most points wins.

OPTIONS/ALTERNATIVES (10–15 minutes)

- For a simpler version of the game, have students only take one card per turn. They get one point for a correct sentence and no points for an incorrect sentence. For this alternative, don't use the *Lose a turn* cards.

Answer Key (Possible responses)

People had already ordered the book online before it became available in stores.

By the time someone said Dr. Jones was the professor, I had already called her by her first name.

When winter officially started, it had already snowed 5 centimeters.

I had lived in the apartment for only a year when I moved again.

We'd already paid for the hotel by the time we arrived.

After he had studied for four hours, Paul decided to take a break.

Jackie had studied biology with me before we worked together.

The thief had already left when Kim realized her wallet was missing.

We hadn't yet left the house when the phone rang.

He had already learned to cook before he moved into his own apartment.

When the children went to school, they hadn't yet eaten breakfast.

The TV program had been popular for five years before it was cancelled.

Jenny had taken knitting lessons for a month before she finally learned how to knit. It had already gotten dark by the time the family ate dinner.

They had been married for less than two years when their first child was born.

LESSON PLAN

First: People ordered the book online.
Second: The book became available in stores.

First: I called Dr. Jones by her first name.
Second: Someone said she was the professor.

First: It snowed 5 centimeters.
Second: Winter officially started.

First: I lived in the apartment for only a year.
Second: I moved again.

First: We paid for the hotel.
Second: We arrived at the hotel.

First: Paul studied for four hours.
Second: Paul decided to take a break.

First: Jackie studied biology with me.
Second: Jackie and I worked together.

First: The thief left.
Second: Kim realized her wallet was missing.

First: We didn't leave the house.
Second: The phone rang.

First: He learned to cook.
Second: He moved into his own apartment.

First: The children didn't eat breakfast.
Second: The children went to school.

First: The TV program was popular for five years.
Second: The TV program was cancelled.

First: Jenny took knitting lessons for a month.
Second: Jenny finally learned how to knit.

First: It got dark.
Second: The family ate dinner.

First: They were married for less than two years.
Second: Their first child was born.

Lose a turn. (Your turn is over. You get 0 points for any sentences you have made on this turn.)

Lose a turn. (Your turn is over. You get 0 points for any sentences you have made on this turn.)

Lose a turn. (Your turn is over. You get 0 points for any sentences you have made on this turn.)

Lose a turn. (Your turn is over. You get 0 points for any sentences you have made on this turn.)

Activity 3   GROUP WORK – Trivia game

UNIT 1 – LESSON 3

Target Language	Materials
Being culturally literate; manners and etiquette vocabulary	Each group needs one copy of the worksheet cut into cards, scrap paper for keeping score, pens or pencils

PREPARATION (5 minutes)

- Read aloud the manners and etiquette definitions on Student's Book page 8. Have students say the correct vocabulary word aloud after you read the definition.

- Invite students to give examples of etiquette in your country or another one. For example, *In this country, it's customary to kiss people when you greet them. In Great Britain it's impolite to arrive late to a meeting.*

PROCEDURE (15 minutes)

- Have students form groups of two, three, or four. One player mixes up the cards within each set and places them facedown in two different piles—one pile of one-point cards, and another pile of two-point cards. (The number on the card indicates the number of points.)

- Explain the activity: The first player decides whether he or she wants to draw a card worth one or two points. (One-point questions are easier, based on information in the unit. Two-point questions are more difficult, based on specific examples of etiquette in specific cultures.) The player to his or her right takes a card from the corresponding pile and reads the card aloud.

- **Note:** Two-point cards are just for fun. Don't expect students to know the answers—they'll learn this cultural etiquette while playing the game.

- If the player answers *True* or *False* correctly, he or she gets the corresponding number of points. Players keep score as they play.

- Play continues among all players as described above.

- The first player to get ten points wins.

OPTIONS/ALTERNATIVES (15–20 minutes)

- Instead of having students choose the difficulty level for each turn, have them mix all of the cards together and play as above, but with one pile of cards.

6 ■ LESSON PLAN

❶ <u>Etiquette</u> refers to the rules of polite behavior in society or in a particular group.

(True.)

---

❶ Different cultures and places have different rules of etiquette.

(True.)

---

❶ If you aren't sure how to address someone, you can ask what the person would like to be called.

(True.)

---

❶ Using a person's first name is usually less formal than using a person's title and last name.

(True.)

---

❶ You can make small talk with a person to get to know him or her better.

(True.)

---

❶ <u>Punctuality</u> refers to respecting the cultures of others.

(False. It refers to the habit of being on time.)

---

❶ If you want to be culturally literate, you should try to be impolite in every culture.

(False. You should be polite.)

---

❶ The *wai* is a customary greeting in Brazil.

(False. The *wai* is a customary greeting in Thailand.)

---

❶ If something is offensive in a culture, then it's good etiquette to do it.

(False. Don't do anything considered offensive.)

---

❶ If you are on a first-name basis with someone, then you probably don't use their title when you talk to them.

(True.)

---

❶ In today's world, cultural literacy is essential to success and good relations with others.

(True.)

---

❷ It is taboo to eat beef in some cultures.

(True. For example, beef is taboo in Hindu cultures because the cow is sacred.)

---

❷ It is considered impolite to show the soles of your feet in Russia.

(True. They are considered very dirty.)

---

❷ It is offensive to give white flowers to a person in Taiwan.

(True. White flowers are generally for funerals.)

---

❷ Handshakes and kisses are customary greetings in Spain.

(True.)

---

❷ In Laos, it is customary to take off your shoes before you enter a person's home.

(True.)

---

❷ In Venezuela, you should call people by their titles until they tell you to use their first names.

(True.)

---

❷ Punctuality is generally important in Great Britain.

(True.)

---

❷ It is good table manners to put your elbows on the table in the U. S.

(False. It is bad table manners.)

---

❷ The number 4 is considered a lucky number in China.

(False. This number is considered unlucky in China.)

---

❷ It is taboo to be late for social events in Mexico.

(False. Punctuality is not extremely important for social events.)

---

❷ In Saudi Arabia, it is impolite to eat with your right hand.

(False. The <u>left</u> hand is considered unclean. Try not to use it.)

---

❷ In Egypt, it is polite to eat everything on your plate.

(False. It's a compliment to leave food on your plate.)

---

❷ It is taboo to greet people with a bow in many Asian countries.

(False. It is customary in many Asian countries.)

Activity 4 — PAIR WORK – Survey; WHOLE CLASS – Discussion

UNIT 1 – LESSON 4

Target Language	Materials
Discussing how culture changes over time	One copy of the worksheet cut in half for each pair of students, pens or pencils

PREPARATION (5 minutes)

- Write the following sentence on the board: *Formal table manners are unnecessary.* Call on a volunteer to say whether he or she agrees or disagrees with the sentence. Ask the student to explain his or her answer. Encourage other students to share their opinions as well.

- As much as possible, prompt students to say more. For example, ask *In general, do you think today's dinner etiquette is impolite? Which table manner do you think are very important? Which do you think aren't very important?* Allow students to ask each other questions to facilitate the conversation.

- Depending on the length of the first discussion, you may repeat the activity with the following sentence: *It is better to use first names at work than titles.*

PROCEDURE (10–15 minutes)

- Have students form pairs. Distribute one survey to each student.

- Explain the activity: Student A reads aloud the first statement. Student B says whether he or she agrees or disagrees with the statement. Student A records Student B's answer on his or her survey form. Encourage students to give reasons to explain their opinions. Student A should take notes on Student B's opinions below the statements. Partners continue in this way until Student B has given his or her opinion on each statement.

- Students switch roles: Student B reads the sentences, and Student A gives his or her opinions.

- Encourage partners to ask one another follow-up questions to learn more information about their answers.

- After partners have completed their surveys, reconvene the class. Tally the responses to each statement. Encourage students to share with the class reasons for their or their partner's opinions.

OPTIONS/ALTERNATIVES (15–20 minutes)

- Have students form groups of three, four, or five students. Cut the surveys into sentence strips. Distribute one set of sentence strips to each group. One student mixes up the strips and puts them in a pile facedown.

- Explain the activity: One group member takes the first strip and reads the statement aloud. The student says whether he or she agrees or disagrees with the statement and gives a reason to explain his or her opinion.

- Then each group member takes a turn giving his or her opinion on the same statement and giving reasons to support it.

- Encourage group members to ask one another follow-up questions to learn more information about their answers.

- The goal of the activity is to prompt discussion. As long as students are conducting their conversations in English, it's OK if they don't get through all of the strips.

Read these statements to your partner.	Your partner's response
Traditions aren't as important to most people as they used to be.	☐ agree ☐ disagree
My musical tastes are different from those of most people who are thirty years older than me.	☐ agree ☐ disagree
Parents, not teachers, should teach children etiquette.	☐ agree ☐ disagree
Dating customs haven't changed a lot since our parents were dating.	☐ agree ☐ disagree
The culture in our country has changed too much in the past fifty years.	☐ agree ☐ disagree
Clothing customs will be less modest in the future.	☐ agree ☐ disagree
In our country, women are more respected than men.	☐ agree ☐ disagree
In the past, children used to have better manners than they do now.	☐ agree ☐ disagree
The culture of our country is less conservative than it used to be.	☐ agree ☐ disagree
Every culture changes over time.	☐ agree ☐ disagree

-------- ✂ --------

Read these statements to your partner.	Your partner's response
Traditions aren't as important to most people as they used to be.	☐ agree ☐ disagree
My musical tastes are different from those of most people who are thirty years older than me.	☐ agree ☐ disagree
Parents, not teachers, should teach children etiquette.	☐ agree ☐ disagree
Dating customs haven't changed a lot since our parents were dating.	☐ agree ☐ disagree
The culture in our country has changed too much in the past fifty years.	☐ agree ☐ disagree
Clothing customs will be less modest in the future.	☐ agree ☐ disagree
In our country, women are more respected than men.	☐ agree ☐ disagree
In the past, children used to have better manners than they do now.	☐ agree ☐ disagree
The culture of our country is less conservative than it used to be.	☐ agree ☐ disagree
Every culture changes over time.	☐ agree ☐ disagree

PHOTOCOPIABLE

Activity 5   GROUP WORK – Charades

Unit 2 – Lesson 1

Target Language	Materials
Must	One copy of the worksheet cut into cards for each group of students

PREPARATION (3–4 minutes)

- Choose a volunteer. Secretly tell the student to act tired (pantomime yawning, falling asleep, etc.). Then say *You must be tired*.
- Pantomime the following sentences yourself: *You're happy.* Then: *You're exercising.* After each pantomime, ask *How do you think I feel? What do you think I'm doing?* Guide students to make the following conclusions: *You must be happy. You must be exercising.*

PROCEDURE (10–15 minutes)

- Have students form groups of three, four, or five. Someone in each group mixes up the cards and places them facedown in a pile.
- Explain the game: The first player chooses a card and silently reads the sentence. Then the player uses pantomime to act out the sentence. For example, if the player draws the *You're sad* card, he or she might make a sad face, pretend to cry, and blow his or her nose.
- Other players make conclusions with *must* about what the person is feeling or doing. (*You must be sad.*) (**Note:** the conclusion must be formed in a grammatically correct sentence.)
- Point out to students that cards may contain actions, feelings, or situations.
- The first player to make a correct conclusion with *must* goes next. He or she chooses another card, and play continues as described above until there are no more cards left.

OPTIONS/ALTERNATIVES (5–10 minutes)

- Divide the class into Teams A and B. Give each team a pile of six cards, facedown.
- Start a timer. Students in Team A take turns acting out the sentences and making guesses. Stop the timer when six correct conclusions are made. Then play switches to Team B.
- The team who made six correct conclusions in the shorter amount of time wins.

Answer Key

Students might act out the sentences as follows:

You have a toothache. Touch cheek, wince in pain, gently touch a tooth.

You're hungry. Rub belly, open refrigerator and look for food, eat very quickly.

You're listening to music. Put on headphones, move to beat, snap fingers.

You're cold. Shiver, rub hands together, blow on hands, put on a sweater.

You're meeting someone (for the first time). Smile, indicate self, as if saying *My name is . . .*, shake hands.

You're late. Look at watch, run, drive quickly, honk horn.

You're angry. Make an angry face, pound fist on something.

You're watching a movie. Stare up at screen, eat popcorn.

You're sad. Make a sad face, cry, blow nose.

You're shopping. Push a cart, pull product off shelf, look at it, put it in cart.

You're nervous. Pace, wring hands, breathe deeply.

You're looking for something. Open drawers, go through piles, turn things over.

You have a toothache.	You're angry.
You're hungry.	You're watching a movie.
You're listening to music.	You're sad.
You're cold.	You're shopping.
You're meeting someone (for the first time).	You're nervous.
You're late.	You're looking for something.

Activity 6 — GROUP WORK – Bingo game

Unit 2 – Lesson 2

Target Language	Materials
Symptoms vocabulary; medical procedures vocabulary	Each student needs one worksheet cut into picture cards, a blank piece of paper, about sixteen markers (small candies, little pieces of crumpled paper, beads, beans, etc.), glue or tape. Each group needs one set of sentence cards.

PREPARATION (2–3 minutes)

- Pretend that you're coughing. Ask students to name the symptom you have.
- Secretly tell a volunteer to act out sneezing. Invite students to name the symptom.
- Continue with a few other symptoms from Student's Book page 16.

PROCEDURE (15–20 minutes)

- Have students form groups of three, four, or five. Distribute a set of picture cards to each student.
- Instruct students to tape their picture cards to a piece of paper in a 4 × 4 grid to make a bingo board. The pictures may be in any order.
- Give a set of sentence cards to one student in each group. He or she mixes up the sentence cards. This student is the "reader."
- Explain the game: The "reader" chooses a sentence card and reads the sentence aloud. (The reader only reads in this round and does not play with a bingo board.)
- The other players each put a marker on the picture that corresponds to the sentence. For example, if the reader chooses *He's been sneezing*, each player puts a marker on his or her picture of the man sneezing.
- The reader chooses another sentence card and reads the sentence aloud. Play continues as described above.
- The first player to have four squares covered in a row (up/down, across, or diagonally) wins.

OPTIONS/ALTERNATIVES (10–15 minutes)

- Players switch roles so that another student reads the sentences. Students exchange bingo boards and play again.
- As an alternative to having one "reader," students take turns picking and reading sentences. All students place markers on their bingo boards in each round.

LESSON PLAN

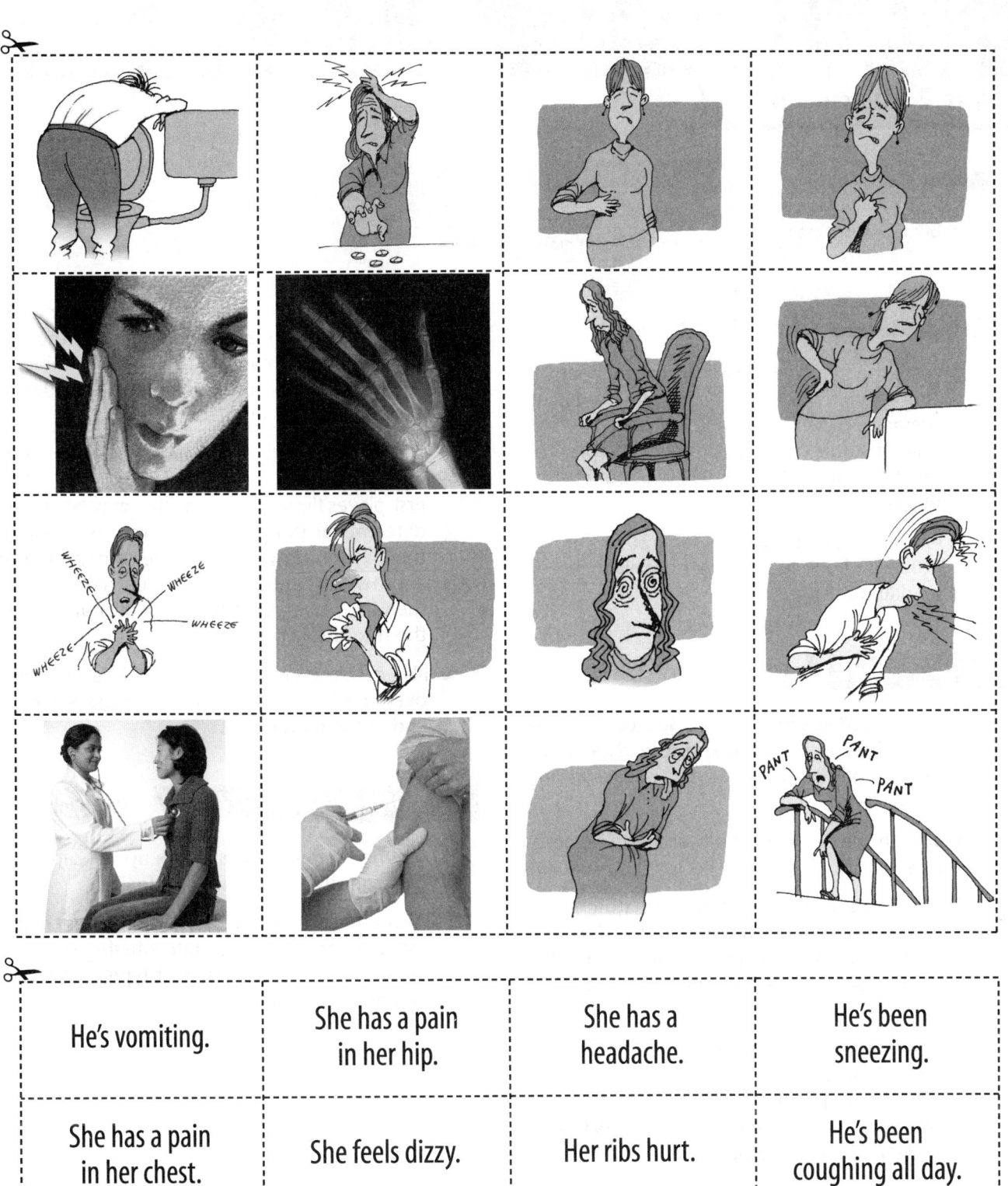

He's vomiting.	She has a pain in her hip.	She has a headache.	He's been sneezing.
She has a pain in her chest.	She feels dizzy.	Her ribs hurt.	He's been coughing all day.
She has a toothache.	He is getting an X-ray.	He's wheezing.	She's having a checkup.
She feels weak.	He's getting a shot.	She has a pain in her stomach.	She's short of breath.

PHOTOCOPIABLE COPY & GO 3 ACTIVITY 6

Activity 7 — PAIR WORK – Concentration

UNIT 2 – LESSON 3

Target Language	Materials
Types of medical treatments	One copy of the worksheet cut into cards for each group of students

PREPARATION (5 minutes)

- Write the following headings on the board: *conventional medicine, homeopathy, herbal therapy, acupuncture, spiritual healing.* Call on students to add under the appropriate heading any details they know about each type of treatment.
- Allow students to refer to page 20 in the Student's Book to add other details they read about.

PROCEDURE (10–15 minutes)

- Divide students into pairs. One student in each pair mixes up the cards and spreads them out facedown in a grid with five cards across and three down.
- Explain the game: One player flips over any three cards.
- If the card is a type of medical treatment, the player reads the treatment aloud. If the card is a fact about a type of medical treatment, the player reads the fact and says the type of medical treatment that it describes.
- If the three cards make a set (one card with a type of medical treatment and two cards with facts about that kind of treatment), then the player picks up these three cards, sets them aside, and takes another turn.
- If the cards do not make a set, then the player turns the cards over again and returns them to their original positions. As much as possible, players should try to remember the location of each card as it is flipped over.
- The next player flips over any three cards. Any of the cards may be the same as the ones the first player flipped over, or they may be three different cards. Again, if the cards make a set, the player picks up these three cards and takes another turn. If the cards do not make a set, then the player turns the cards over and returns them to their original positions.
- Play continues in this way until all cards have been used. The player with the most sets at the end of the game wins.

OPTIONS/ALTERNATIVES (10–15 minutes)

- As time permits, students mix up the cards, make another grid, and play again.
- Each time a player successfully matches three cards, he or she should state whether or not he or she would ever use that type of treatment and give a reason.

conventional medicine	This type of treatment is based on scientific study of the human body and illness.	This type of treatment had its beginnings in ancient Greece.
homeopathy	In this type of treatment, the patient's symptoms are treated with remedies that cause similar symptoms.	This type of treatment began in Germany in the late 1700s.
herbal therapy	80% of the world's population uses this type of treatment.	In this type of treatment, patients take herbs, often as teas or pills.
acupuncture	This type of treatment began in China over 5,000 years ago.	Needles are inserted at certain points on the body in this type of treatment.
spiritual healing	This type of treatment uses the mind or religious faith to treat illness.	This type of treatment is also known as mind and body connection.

PHOTOCOPIABLE

Activity 8 — GROUP WORK – Conversation

Unit 2 – Lesson 4

Target Language	Materials
Making an appointment; describing symptoms at a doctor's office	One copy of the worksheet cut into strips for each group of students

PREPARATION (2–3 minutes)

- Write the following sentences on the board:
  I'd like to make an appointment.
  Is anything bothering you today?
  You must feel terrible.
  My tooth is killing me.

- Ask students who would probably say each sentence and to whom. (For example, a patient to a receptionist, a doctor to a patient, etc.)

- Invite students to suggest responses to each sentence.

PROCEDURE (15–20 minutes)

- Put students in groups of two to five students.

- Explain the activity: Each group receives nine text strips. Each strip contains a sentence or phrase. Each group has ten minutes to prepare a short conversation or role play for the class. The conversation may be about any topic and can include any characters. The only rule is that it must include the nine sentences or phrases from the strips. Students may incorporate these into the conversation in any way they like.

- Encourage students to be creative, perhaps using the sentences in unexpected ways.

- Invite groups to present their conversations to the rest of the class. During the performance, students hold up the corresponding strip each time they say one of the nine sentences or phrases.

OPTIONS/ALTERNATIVES (15 minutes)

- For a quicker version of this activity, distribute only three or four text strips to each group to incorporate into a conversation. Give different combinations of strips to each group.

- Have students vote to decide which group made the most original conversation.

16 ■ LESSON PLAN

Let's see if I can fit you in.

coughing and sneezing

herbal therapy

a shot

antacid

I think it's an emergency.

That must be painful.

My _____ is killing me.

I really appreciate it.

Activity 9 GROUP WORK: Sentence – creation card game

UNIT 3 – LESSON 1

Target Language	Materials
Causatives <u>get</u>, <u>have</u>, and <u>make</u>; some ways to help out another person	Each group needs one copy of the worksheet (cut into a grid and two sets of cards), a timer or watch that can measure seconds, a coin or other small object, scrap paper for keeping score, pen or pencil

PREPARATION (3–5 minutes)

- Write the following information on the board:

they	make	him	clean up
we	get	us	make 100 copies
I	have	my sister	bring the food

- Draw lines to connect *they, have, us,* and *bring the food*. Make a sentence with a causative: *They had us bring the food to the party.*

- Erase the lines and draw new lines to connect *I, get, my sister,* and *make 100 copies*. Make the sentence *I got my sister to make 100 copies of the brochure.*

- Continue to draw lines to make different combinations. Call on students to use the words to make sentences with a causative. Encourage them to add their own endings, such as *after the party*, as appropriate.

PROCEDURE (10–15 minutes)

- Put students in groups of three, four, or five. One student mixes up the cards within each set and places them facedown in two piles.

- Explain the activity: One player starts the timer for any amount of time between 20 and 45 seconds. He or she is the moderator in this round and does not play.

- The player to his or her left picks up one card from each pile and then tosses a coin (or other small object) onto the grid. The player uses the cards and the phrase from the grid to make a sentence with a causative. For example, if the player picks *I / get* and *their classmates* and the coin lands on *give us a ride*, then a correct sentence might be: *I got their classmates to give us a ride to the school.*

- If the sentence is correct, play passes to the next player on the left. He or she takes a card from each pile, tosses the coin onto the grid, and makes a sentence as explained above.

- If the sentence is incorrect, the same player tries again, using the same cards. Play does not pass to the next person until the student makes a correct sentence. The moderator is the judge of correct sentences.

- When the indicated amount of time has passed, the moderator *says time*. The student who is making a sentence when *time* is announced gets one point. Students return all used cards to the correct piles and shuffle them.

- Note that the goal of this game is to have the <u>least</u> number of points, so students will try <u>not</u> to be the one whose turn it is when the timer goes off.

- In the next round, the new moderator is the person to the left of the previous one. He or she sets the timer and students play as described above.

- Play continues in this way until each player has been moderator twice. At the end of the game, the player with the <u>least</u> points wins.

OPTIONS / ALTERNATIVES (10–15 minutes)

- Students may play without the timer. They simply take turns picking three cards and using them to make a correct sentence. Students earn one point for each correct sentence they make.

- After all students have had the same number of turns (about five), the student with the most points wins.

18 ■ LESSON PLAN

Set 1 ✂

I / get	She / get	you / have
We / have	They / make	He / make

Set 2 ✂

the students	my brother	his sister
their classmates	your coworker	my assistant
our teacher	me	them

plan the conference	make copies	agree to a new meeting	clean up
bring students to their classrooms	make 100 copies	sign the documents	do the laundry
call them	give us a ride	keep an eye on your books	lend you a pen
fill in for her	pick up the files	help me	finish the assignment

PHOTOCOPIABLE   COPY & GO 3 ■ ACTIVITY 9   19

Activity 10 PAIR WORK – Information gap

UNIT 3 – LESSON 2

Target Language	Materials
The passive causative	One copy of the worksheet cut in half for each pair of students, pens or pencils

PREPARATION (2–3 minutes)

- Write the following information on the board:
  Where / Cassie / papers / copy?   Copy Plus
  Where / Jeff / signs / print?   Sign It!
  Where / Michelle / photos / enlarge? Fantastic Photos

- Model using the first set of words to make the question *Where does Cassie get* (*have*) *papers copied?* Encourage students to answer in complete sentences (*She gets / has papers copied at Copy Plus*).

- Have students make questions and answers with the other sets of words. (*Where does Jeff have / get signs printed? He has / gets them printed at Sign It! Where does Michelle get / have photos enlarged? She gets / has them enlarged at Fantastic Photos.*)

PROCEDURE (10–15 minutes)

- Divide students into pairs. One student gets the Student A half of the worksheet, and the other gets the Student B half.

- Explain the activity: Student A begins by asking a question about where one of the people on the worksheet has a specific service done. (*Where does Conrad get his clothes dry-cleaned?*)

- Student B refers to his or her chart and provides the answer. Student A records the information on his or her chart.

- Student B then asks Student A a question about where someone gets a service done. (*Where does Tom get his clothes dry-cleaned?*) Student A refers to his or her chart and provides the answer.

- Students continue until both partners have completed their charts.

- Students compare charts to check their answers.

OPTIONS / ALTERNATIVES (5 minutes)

- Remind students to spell the names of businesses for their partners if necessary.

- After they have completed their charts, have partners ask each other questions about where <u>they</u> get each service done.

Answer Key

	Tom	Teresa	Conrad	Sylvia
dry-clean clothes	Speedy's	River's Cleaners	Sixth Avenue Cleaners	Local Laundry
repair shoes	Fix It	Corner Cobbler	Robert's Shoe Repair	Step It Up!
process film	Photos Plus	Stan Mart	Photos and More	In and Out Photos
frame pictures	Mike's Craft Shop	Frame It!	Picture Perfect	Fisher's Frames
cut hair	A Cut Above	Shear Joy	Cedrick's	Studio 29

LESSON PLAN

STUDENT A

	Tom	Teresa	Conrad	Sylvia
dry-clean clothes	Speedy's	River's Cleaners	_____	_____
repair shoes	_____	Corner Cobbler	_____	Step It Up!
process film	_____	_____	Photos and More	In and Out Photos
frame pictures	Mike's Craft Shop	_____	Picture Perfect	_____
cut hair	_____	Shear Joy	Cedrick's	_____

STUDENT B

	Tom	Teresa	Conrad	Sylvia
dry-clean clothes	_____	_____	Sixth Avenue Cleaners	Local Laundry
repair shoes	Fix It	_____	Robert's Shoe Repair	_____
process film	Photos Plus	Stan Mart	_____	_____
frame pictures	_____	Frame It!	_____	Fisher's Frames
cut hair	A Cut Above	_____	_____	Studio 29

PHOTOCOPIABLE COPY & GO 3 ■ ACTIVITY 10

Activity 11 GROUP WORK – Card game

Unit 3 – Lesson 3

Target Language	Materials
Evaluating the quality of service	Each pair needs one copy of the worksheet cut into cards, a coin, scrap paper for keeping score, pen or pencil

PREPARATION (5 minutes)

- Refer students to the adjectives in the box in Exercise B on page 33 of the Student's Book.
- Call on students to say which adjectives are most important to them in a service. Invite them to mention other adjective qualities that they value, such as friendly employees or high-quality items.

PROCEDURE (10–15 minutes)

- Have students form pairs (or groups of three or four). One student mixes up the cards and places them facedown in a pile.
- Explain the game: Player A tosses the coin. (Designate one side as *one point* and the other as *two points*.) This determines the number of points the player will get if he or she answers the question correctly.
- Player B takes a card and reads the question and options a–c aloud. If Player A answers correctly, he or she gets the number of points corresponding to the side of the coin flipped. If Player A answers incorrectly, he or she gets zero points. (The ★ symbol indicates the correct answer.)
- Students keep score as they play.
- Students switch roles. Player B tosses the coin, and Player A reads a question.
- Anytime a *Lose a turn* card is drawn, the player's turn is immediately over and he or she gets zero points.
- Play continues as described above. The first player to get ten points wins.

OPTIONS/ALTERNATIVES (10–15 minutes)

- Have students form teams and play in groups instead of in pairs.
- Teams discuss the answer to each question. They must come to a consensus before they announce their answer.

22 ■ LESSON PLAN

Which place is known for custom-made clothes? a. Hong Kong ★ b. Great Britain c. Costa Rica	What do you have to pay before a tailor begins a custom-made garment? a. a deposit ★ b. a tax c. a monogram	If you are not satisfied with the finished product, ___. a. you have to accept it b. you don't have to accept it ★ c. you get your deposit back
A custom-made item is made ___. a. especially for you ★ b. in a factory c. by hand	You can't have a tailor make ___. a. cashmere ★ b. a formal dress c. a suit	What does a tailor need in order to make clothes for you? a. your garments b. your measurements ★ c. your finished product
It will take about ___ to have a garment custom-made. a. three to five days ★ b. one to two weeks c. three to five weeks	If a business is reliable, then the workers ___. a. keep their promises ★ b. work quickly c. charge a lot of money	Once your tailor has your ___, you most likely will be able to order more clothing online. a. deposit b. suit c. measurements ★
Custom-made clothing should ___. a. fit you perfectly ★ b. come from Hong Kong c. be made in 24 hours	Reasonable prices are ___. a. fair prices ★ b. too much money c. more expensive	Who can lengthen or shorten a skirt? a. a courier service b. a tailor ★ c. a stylist
A professional business has ___ service. a. no b. long c. very good ★	Tailors in Hong Kong are willing to try to make almost any garment you want, even if the request is a bit unusual. They are very ___. a. helpful ★ b. reliable c. reasonable	At your first ___, the tailor will take your measurements. a. deposit b. fitting ★ c. garment
Lose a turn.	Lose a turn.	Lose a turn.

PHOTOCOPIABLE

COPY & GO 3 ■ ACTIVITY 11   23

Activity 12 — GROUP WORK – Bingo game

UNIT 3 – LESSON 4

Target Language	Materials
Planning an event	Each student needs one copy of the worksheet cut into picture cards, a blank piece of paper, about nine markers (small candies, little pieces of crumpled paper, beads, beans, etc.), glue or tape. Each group needs one set of sentence cards.

PREPARATION (5 minutes)

- Invite students to name some of the steps involved in planning an event. If necessary, prompt them with clues, such as *You have to get someone to do the music. You have to decide how to spend the money. You have get the room ready for the party,* etc.

PROCEDURE (10 minutes)

- Have students form groups of three, four, or five. Distribute a set of picture cards to each student.
- Instruct students to tape their picture cards to a piece of paper in a 3 × 3 grid to make a bingo board. The pictures may be in any order.
- Give a set of sentence cards to one student in each group. He or she mixes them up. This student is the "reader."
- Explain the game: The "reader" chooses a sentence card and reads the sentence aloud. (The reader only reads in this round and does not play with a bingo board.)
- The other players each put a marker on the picture that corresponds to the sentence. For example, if the reader chooses *Have you arranged the caterer yet?*, each player puts a marker on his or her picture of the caterer.
- The reader chooses another sentence card and reads the sentence aloud. Play continues as described above.
- The first player to have three squares covered in a row (up/down, across, or diagonally) wins.

OPTIONS/ALTERNATIVES (5–10 minutes)

- Players switch roles so that another student reads the sentences. Students exchange bingo boards and play again.
- As an alternative, students take turns picking and reading sentences. All students place markers on their bingo boards in each round.

Have you arranged catering yet?	Let's make a list of attendees for the party.	We have to decide what time to have the event.
Did you already send out the announcements?	We still have to plan the agenda.	Let's assign some responsibilities to people.
We need to pick a place for the party.	Who's going to set up the room?	We need to make a budget for the event.

PHOTOCOPIABLE

COPY & GO 3 ■ ACTIVITY 12 25

Activity 13 GROUP WORK – Guessing game

UNIT 4 – LESSON 1

Target Language	Materials
Noun clauses	One set of question cards for each group of students, ten blank strips of paper for each student, pens or pencils

PREPARATION (5 minutes)

- Write the following question on the board: *Which magazine do you think is the most interesting?*

- Call on volunteers to use *I think . . . , I believe . . . ,* or *I guess . . .* and a noun clause to answer the question. For example: *I think (that) News is the most interesting magazine. I believe (that) Fix Everything is the most interesting. I guess (that) Maximum is pretty interesting.*

- Prompt students to give a little more information about their answers. For example, ask *Why do you think [News] is the most interesting?*

- Have students use noun clauses to answer the following questions:
What is something that you hope your children do / don't do?
What do you think is the best movie ever made?

PROCEDURE (10–15 minutes)

- Put students in groups of at least four. One student mixes up the question cards and places them facedown in a pile.

- Explain the activity: One student takes a card and reads the question aloud. Each student writes his or her own answer on a blank strip of paper.

- Students must use a noun clause as a direct object in each answer. For example, if the question is *What is something that you think is a waste of money?*, students might write *I think fancy cars are a waste of money* or *I guess that sometimes new clothes are a waste of money, but I buy them anyway.*

- The student who reads the question collects the sentences and mixes them up. One by one he or she reads the responses aloud. Group members try to guess who wrote each sentence.

- As appropriate, encourage students to ask one another questions to learn more about their answers. As long as students conduct their conversations in English, it's OK if they don't get through all of the questions.

OPTIONS / ALTERNATIVES (5 minutes)

- Have students think of their own questions. Remind them to use verbs such as *think, (don't) know, hope, guess,* and *believe* in their questions. Play continues as above.

What do you hope will happen in the future?	What do you believe everyone should learn?
What is one book that you think is really good?	What do you hope won't happen in the future?
What is something that you think is a waste of money?	What is one thing you don't think is good for the environment?
What do you think is the best restaurant in this area?	What do you believe is important to teach children?
When you were a child, what did you hope you would be?	What is something that you didn't know when you were young?

Activity 14   GROUP WORK – Questions and answers

UNIT 4 – LESSON 2

Target Language	Materials
Noun clauses: embedded questions	Each group needs one copy of the worksheet cut into cards, a pen or pencil, scrap paper for keeping score

PREPARATION   (5 minutes)

- Write on the board the following clauses:
  Tell me who . . .
  Do you know where . . .
  Could you tell me whether . . .

- Use the clauses to ask students embedded questions. For example, *Tell me who sings the song "[Heartbreak Hotel]." Do you know where the author [Gabriel Garcia Marquez] is from? Could you tell me whether [The Economist] is a weekly magazine?* Call on students to answer the questions.

- Invite students to use the clauses to make a few embedded questions of their own.

PROCEDURE   (15 minutes)

- Put students in groups of three to six. One student in each group mixes up the cards and places them facedown in a pile.

- Explain the game: The first player takes a card and uses the clause on the card to make an embedded question. He or she earns one point for forming a correct question.

- The player to his or her left has the chance to earn one point by correctly answering the question. If he or she answers incorrectly, the next player to the left then has the chance to answer for one point.

- Play continues in the same direction until someone answers correctly. If no one is able to answer the question, the student who asked the question says the correct answer. Students keep track of their points. The card is set aside.

- Play continues in a clockwise direction, with the next player drawing a card and asking a question.

- Players can try to "stump" one another with difficult questions so other players do not earn points for answering. However, players must know the answers to the questions they ask.

- Play continues until all the cards have been used. The player with the most points wins.

OPTIONS / ALTERNATIVES   (15 minutes)

- For a more exciting alternative, allow players to answer any question they know the answer to, not necessarily in turn. The first person to answer a question correctly gets the point.

- For an easier alternative, divide students into two teams. Distribute half of the cards to each team. Teams have 5 minutes to complete the embedded questions on their cards. They may write directly on the cards.

- Teams take turns asking and answering each other's questions. (One point is awarded for forming a correct embedded question; another is given for a correct answer.)

- After all cards have been read, the team with the most points wins.

Tell me why . . .	I've been wondering who . . .	I wonder if . . .
Tell me when . . .	I wonder why . . .	Can you tell me where . . .
Could you tell me whether . . .	Tell me who . . .	I'd like to know what . . .
I wonder who . . .	Do you know why . . .	Tell me what . . .
Do you know where . . .	Tell me if . . .	Can you tell me who . . .
Do you know whether . . .	Can you tell me when . . .	I wonder what . . .
I wonder where . . .	Do you know when . . .	Could you tell me what . . .
Do you know what . . .	Can you tell me why . . .	Tell me where . . .
I don't know if . . .	I'd like to know where . . .	Could you tell me where . . .

Activity 15 WHOLE CLASS – Find someone who . . .

UNIT 4 – LESSON 3

Target Language	Materials
Describing reading habits; some ways to enjoy reading vocabulary	One half worksheet per student, pens or pencils

PREPARATION (2–3 minutes)

- Ask several students questions such as the following:
  Do you read science fiction?
  How often do you read magazines?
  Have you ever read a memoir?
  Do you like thrillers?

- Ask follow-up questions, such as:
  Can you tell me which science fiction you have read?
  Tell me your favorite magazine.

PROCEDURE (10–15 minutes)

- Distribute half of a worksheet to each student. You may choose to give all students the same half of the worksheet, or, for variety, you can give the top half to some students and the bottom half to others.

- Explain the activity: Students ask one another questions about the reading habits on their worksheets. For example, *Do you enjoy novels?* When they find someone who answers in the affirmative, they write his or her name on the first line in that row.

- Students then ask for additional information about that reading habit and fill in the second line in the row. Encourage students to use embedded questions whenever possible: *Can you tell me who your favorite author is?*

- Encourage students to circulate around the classroom to talk to as many people as possible.

- After students have completed their worksheets, reconvene the class. Invite students to share information they learned about their classmates' reading habits.

OPTIONS/ALTERNATIVES (10–15 minutes)

- Have students add their own follow-up questions, such as *Can you tell me what your favorite novels are? Tell me who your favorite mystery writer is.*

Find someone who...	Name	Details
• reads articles online.	_____	What kind? _____
• enjoys novels.	_____	A favorite author? _____
• reads the newspaper.	_____	How often? _____
• thinks self-help books are useful.	_____	Which ones? _____
• listens to audio books.	_____	When? _____
• skims through some reading materials.	_____	What kind of materials? _____
• reads mysteries.	_____	Why? _____

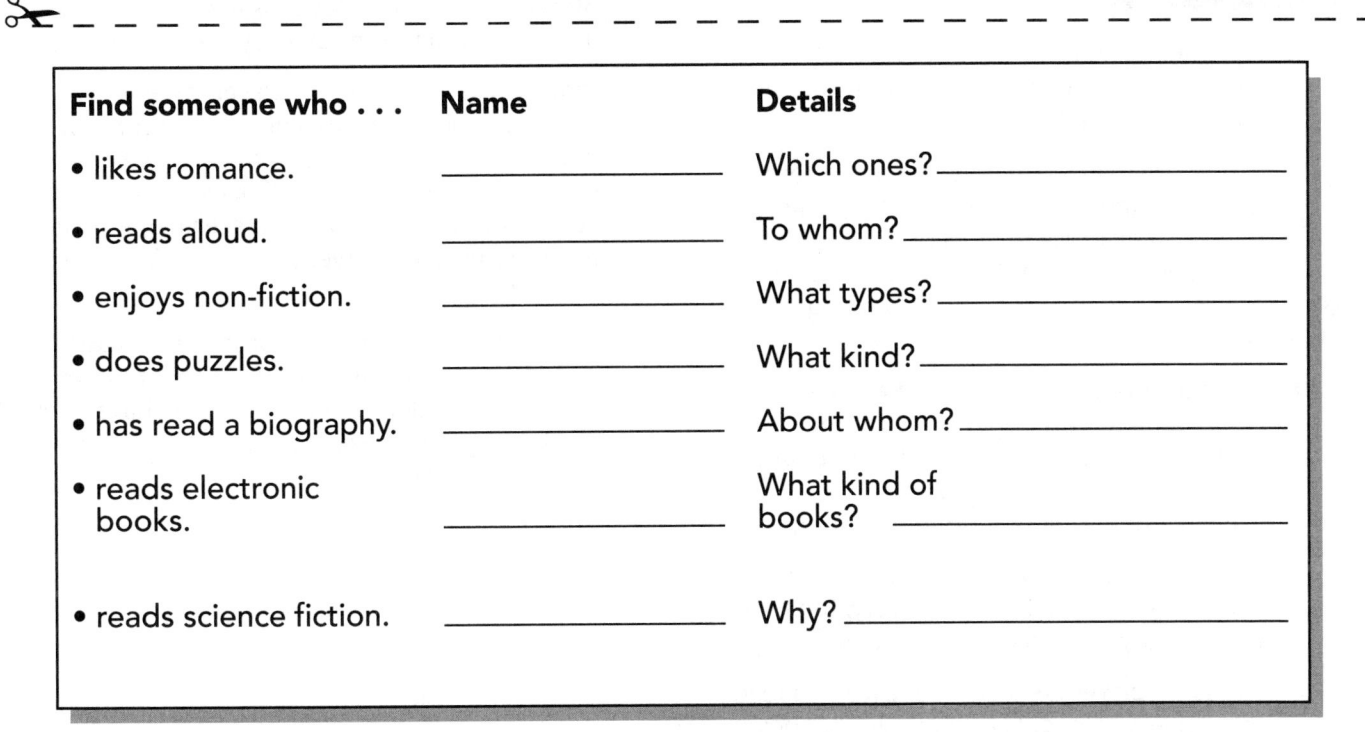

✂ -

Find someone who...	Name	Details
• likes romance.	_____	Which ones? _____
• reads aloud.	_____	To whom? _____
• enjoys non-fiction.	_____	What types? _____
• does puzzles.	_____	What kind? _____
• has read a biography.	_____	About whom? _____
• reads electronic books.	_____	What kind of books? _____
• reads science fiction.	_____	Why? _____

PHOTOCOPIABLE

Activity 16 GROUP WORK – Reading materials game

UNIT 4 – LESSON 4

Target Language	Materials
Types of reading materials; discussing the quality of reading materials	Each group needs one copy of the worksheet cut into cards, scrap paper, a pen or pencil

PREPARATION (3–4 minutes)

- Have students look at the types of books and other reading materials on Student's Book pages 38 and 47.
- Call on students to name specific titles from various categories that they like or dislike. Invite them to say why they feel the way they do.

PROCEDURE (10–15 minutes)

- Put students in groups of four to six. One student mixes up the cards and sets them facedown in a pile.
- Explain the game: One player takes a card and reads the sentence aloud. He or she names an example to fit the category on the card. For example, if the card is *Name one type of non-fiction book*, the player might say *biography*.
- The player passes the card to the player on his or her left. This player gives another example to fit the category. Play continues around the circle until a player is unable to give another original example.
- When a player is unable to think of a new correct example to fit the category, the round ends. That player receives one point.
- The same player takes another card and reads the sentence aloud. Play continues as above until all the cards have been used. The player with the <u>fewest</u> points wins.

OPTIONS/ALTERNATIVES (10–15 minutes)

- For this alternative, each group needs one worksheet cut into cards, a timer that measures seconds or a watch with a second hand, one sheet of blank paper per student, and pens or pencils.
- One player mixes up the cards and places them facedown in a pile. He or she chooses a card and reads the sentence aloud.
- The player begins the timer. All players have 30 seconds to write down as many examples as they can to fit the category on the card.
- When 30 seconds are up, players take turns reading their responses aloud. If two (or more) players wrote the same response, they both cross it off their list. After all players have compared their lists, players receive one point for every unique answer they have. The card is set aside.
- The next player chooses another card, reads it aloud, and sets the timer. Play continues as above. When all the cards in the pile have been used, the game is over. The player with the most points wins.

Name a character in a comic book.	Name a character in a mystery.
Name a novel that students often have to read in school.	Name a magazine that is sold in this country.
Name a type of reading material that some people think is trash.	Name one type of non-fiction book.
Name a newspaper that is sold in this country.	Name a book that was written by an author from this country.
Name one type of fiction book.	Name a comic book that is sold in this country.

Activity 17 — GROUP WORK – Charades

UNIT 5 – LESSON 1

Target Language	Materials
Indirect speech: imperatives	Each group needs one copy of the worksheet cut into cards

PREPARATION (3 minutes)

- Invite several volunteers to the front of the room. One by one, secretly give them commands such as *turn down the radio, don't get dressed, go to bed,* etc. Students act out each command. (They can portray negative commands by first drawing the international "no" symbol (Ø) on the board and then pantomiming the action.)

- The class guesses what you told each student to do. For example, *You said to turn down the radio. You said not to get dressed. You said to go to bed.*

PROCEDURE (15 minutes)

- Put students in groups of four, five, or six. A student in each group mixes up the cards and places them facedown in a pile.

- Explain the game: In each round, one group member is the "teller" and one is the "actor." The teller chooses a card and silently reads the command on the card. The teller whispers the command to the actor.

- The actor uses pantomime to act out the command. For example, if the teller takes the *Watch TV* card, then he or she whispers to the actor *Watch TV*. The actor pantomimes watching TV (picking up the remote, turning on the TV, leaning back in a chair, flipping channels, etc.).

- The actor can draw the Ø symbol on a piece of paper to preface negative commands, as described above.

- Other group members try to guess what the teller told the actor to do. They use indirect speech to say what they think the command was. (*He or she said to watch TV.*)

- The first player to correctly say the command in indirect speech is the next actor. The actor from the last round is now the teller. He or she takes another card and whispers a command to the actor.

- Play continues as above until there are no more cards left.

OPTIONS/ALTERNATIVES (5 minutes)

- Have groups of students play against one another. Give each group a set time limit (about 1 minute) to guess as many commands as they can.

- After each group has played for 1 minute, the team that correctly guessed the most commands wins.

Shorten a skirt.	Don't get stuck in traffic.
Play tennis.	Listen to music.
Take medication.	Photocopy something.
Eat something.	Don't weave through traffic.
Do aerobics.	Put on a sweater.
Don't close the window.	Don't go shopping.
Don't miss the bus.	Don't lift weights.
Go skiing.	Don't march in a parade.
Watch TV.	Take a shower.
Clean the house.	Get married.
Relax.	Make breakfast.
Read the newspaper.	Open the door.
Go bike riding.	Wash the dishes.

PHOTOCOPIABLE

Activity 18 GROUP WORK – Board game

UNIT 5 – LESSON 2

Target Language	Materials
Indirect speech: say and tell; tense changes	Each group needs one copy of the worksheet cut into twenty-one cards and a game board, one coin, four place markers (coins, poker chips, etc.)

PREPARATION (3–4 minutes)

- Write the following sentences on the board:
  Mr. Klein: "I've changed my plans."
  The news reporter: "The storm is very strong."
  Henry: "The weather is getting bad."

- Call on volunteers to report each person's speech, using say. (Mr. Klein said (that) he'd changed his plans. The news reporter said (that) the storm was very strong. Henry said (that) the weather was getting bad.)

- Then write the following names after the sentences:
  Mr. Klein: "I've changed my plans." (Ms. Jones)
  The news reporter: "The storm is very strong."
     (the viewers)
  Henry: "The weather is getting bad." (us)

- Have students report the speech again, this time using tell and the name in parentheses. (Mr. Klein told Ms. Jones (that) he'd changed his plans. The news reporter told the viewers (that) the storm was very strong. Henry told us (that) the weather was getting bad.)

PROCEDURE (10–15 minutes)

- Put students in groups of two, three, or four. One student mixes up the cards and places them facedown in a pile. Designate one side of the coin as say and the other as tell.

- Explain the game: All players begin at START. The first player takes a card and reads the sentence aloud. Then he or she flips the coin.

- The player uses the name(s) on the space, the correct verb (say or tell), and the sentence on the card to make a sentence in indirect speech. (The name in parentheses becomes the object of the verb tell. It is not used if the coin lands on the say side.)

- For example, if the player is on the first space, draws the card that reads *The landslide didn't cause any injuries*, and flips the coin to the tell side, then he or she says: *Adam told Daniel (that) the landslide hadn't caused any injuries*.

- The player returns the card to the bottom of the pile.

- If the sentence is correct, the player advances to the next space. On the next turn, he or she will take another card, flip the coin, and make a new sentence with the name(s) on that space.

- If the sentence is incorrect, then the player stays at START. On the next turn, he or she will take another card, flip the coin, and make a new sentence with the name(s) on that space.

- Play continues as above, with each player forming a correct sentence for each space before they can advance to the next space.

- The first student to reach END wins.

OPTIONS/ALTERNATIVES (10 minutes)

- For a faster alternative, allow students to continue their turn after making a correct sentence. They may take up to two extra turns.

- A more challenging alternative is for students to play without the coin. On each turn, they must make two correct sentences, one with say and one with tell, in order to advance to the next space.

Game Board (START to END)

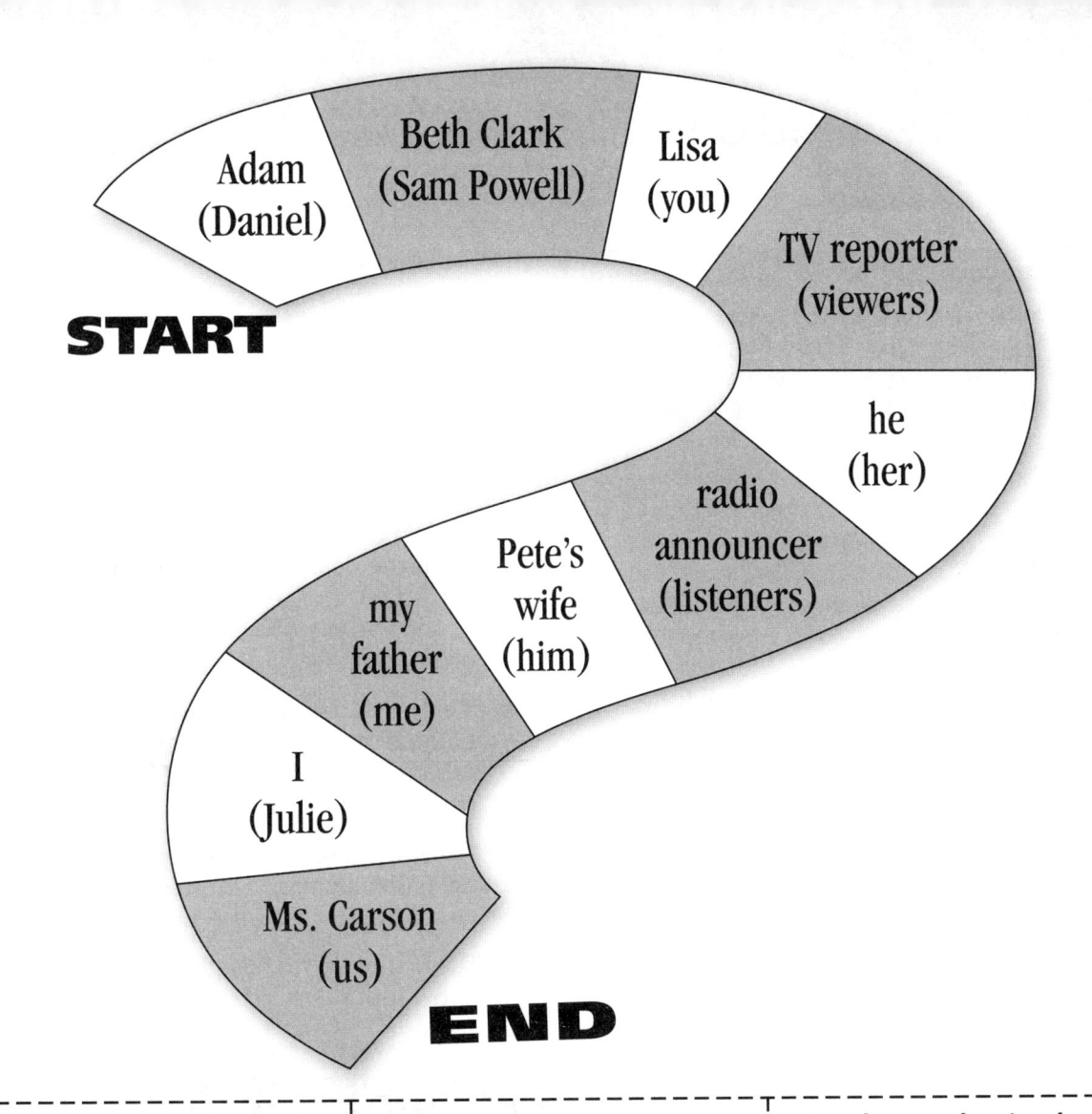

- Adam (Daniel)
- Beth Clark (Sam Powell)
- Lisa (you)
- TV reporter (viewers)
- he (her)
- radio announcer (listeners)
- Pete's wife (him)
- my father (me)
- I (Julie)
- Ms. Carson (us)

"The landslide didn't cause any injuries."	"The main road out of the city is flooded."	"People were buying lots of supplies at the store."
"Watch TV to find out about the storm."	"We don't have electricity because of the storm."	"Hurricane Joan has caused more damage to the city than any other."
"The water from the flood is one meter high."	"Don't try to leave the house."	"You need to change your travel plans."
"I haven't heard about any deaths."	"Get extra food and water before the storm arrives."	"Get vaccinated before you travel to certain places."
"Don't touch any fallen wires or cables after a storm."	"A lot of houses were destroyed by the typhoon."	"Move away from all windows during a tornado."
"It hasn't rained for over five months."	"I'm surprised by the speed of the wind."	"A big storm is coming."
"I'm looking at the latest information available."	"I'm reading the emergency instructions in the newspaper."	"Don't believe everything you hear about the storm."

PHOTOCOPIABLE   COPY & GO 3 ■ ACTIVITY 18

Activity 19 — PAIR WORK – Bingo game

Unit 5 – Lesson 3

Target Language	Materials
Severe weather and other natural disasters vocabulary; adjectives of severity	Each student needs one blank bingo board, about sixteen markers (small candies, little pieces of crumpled paper, beads, beans, etc.), and a pen or pencil. Each pair of students needs one set of Definition Cards.

PREPARATION (3 minutes)

- Students take turns reading aloud the Definition Cards from the worksheeet.
- Class members say the correct vocabulary word after each definition.
- Write the words on the board as students say them.
- The final word list on the board should consist of: *breaking news, casualties, catastrophe, death toll, drought, due to, earthquake, enormous* (or *gigantic* or *huge*), *epidemic, famine, flood, horrendous, hurricane* (or *a typhoon*), *injuries, landslide, magnitude, mild, natural disaster, property damage, tornado.*

PROCEDURE (15–20 minutes)

- Have students form pairs (or groups of three). Distribute a set of Definition Cards to each pair and a blank bingo board and markers to each student.
- Students choose sixteen of the words from the board and write one word in each blank square on their bingo boards. They may write the words in any order they like.
- One student in each pair mixes up the Definition Cards and places them facedown in a pile.
- Explain the game: Player A chooses a card and reads the definition aloud. Player B says the correct vocabulary word. (For example, if Player A reads *people who are not killed when a disaster occurs*, then Player B says *survivors*.)
- If either student has the word on his or her bingo board, he or she puts a marker on the square. If a student doesn't have the word, he or she does nothing.
- Player B chooses another card and reads the definition aloud. Player A says the vocabulary word. Play continues as described above.
- The first player to have four squares covered in a row (up/down, across, or diagonally) wins.

OPTIONS / ALTERNATIVES (10–15 minutes)

- Students exchange bingo boards, shuffle the cards, and play again.
- Depending on your class size, you may also choose to do this game as a whole-class activity.

BINGO

| the number of people, hurt in a disaster |
| a sudden shaking of the earth's surface that often causes a lot of damage |
| very big |
| an expression used to describe the first news reports of an important event that is happening at the present. |
| terrible, causing a lot of damage, destruction, injuries, and/or death |

✂ Definition Cards

The strength of an earthquake that is measured by the Richter scale.	people who are either injured or killed in a disaster	a very violent tropical storm
because of	really bad	a long period of dry weather when there is not enough water for plants and animals to live
a rapid and wide spread of a contagious disease	when there is not enough food for everyone	a sudden fall of a lot of earth or rocks down a hill
loss of buildings, roads, trees, and plants caused by disasters	a disaster caused by nature, not people	a very large amount of water that covers an area that is usually dry
having a small effect, not serious enough to cause much suffering and/or damage	the number of people killed in a disaster	an extremely violent storm consisting of air that spins very quickly and causes a lot of damage

Activity 20 — GROUP WORK – Discussion

Unit 5 – Lesson 4

Target Language	Materials
Emergency preparations and supplies	One copy of the worksheet for each group of students, pens or pencils

PREPARATION (4–5 minutes)

- Present students with the following scenario: *There is a huge storm coming toward [your city or town]. Experts predict there will be very strong winds. They expect the storm to last several days, and you won't be able to leave your house. They say there will be power outages. The wind will be so strong that it will probably break windows. You'll need to stay in your basement for a few days until the storm passes. What things do you think you'll need to have with you in the basement?*

- Invite students to name things they think they would need in this emergency. Record their answers in a list on the board. Provide vocabulary as necessary. Students might suggest items such as *bottled water, blankets, non-perishable food, a can opener, candles, matches, flashlights, batteries, a radio, books, sleeping bags, extra clothes, toilet paper, toothbrushes, games.*

PROCEDURE (10–15 minutes)

- Put students in groups of four or more. Distribute one worksheet to each group.

- Explain the activity: Tell students that they will spend the days of the storm together with their group members in a small basement. The basement is so small that they will be able to take only ten items with them. They have ten minutes to decide which ten things they're going to take and why each one is important.

- Students must also rate the items in order of importance (with 1 being the most important and 10 the least important).

- Students work together to come to a group decision. They may try to convince other group members to change their minds about items or their order of importance.

OPTIONS/ALTERNATIVES (5 minutes)

- After groups have finished their lists, have them share their decisions with the rest of the class.

- Depending on the size of the class, you might conduct the entire exercise as a whole-class activity.

Item	Reason	Order of importance

Activity 21   GROUP WORK – Sentence-creation card game

UNIT 6 – LESSON 1

Target Language	Materials
Was / were going to	Each group needs one copy of the worksheet (cut into three sets of cards), a timer or watch that can measure seconds, scrap paper for keeping score, pen or pencil

PREPARATION (5 minutes)

- Write the following information on the board in three columns:

  Richard   eat dinner at Eli's   affirmative statement
  Vicky   take a trip   negative statement
  they   study medicine   question

- Draw lines to connect *Richard, eat dinner at Eli's,* and *negative statement*. Make a sentence with was / were going to: *Richard wasn't going to eat dinner at Eli's, but he changed his mind.*

- Erase the lines and draw new lines to connect *they, take a trip,* and *question*. Make the sentence *Weren't they going to take a trip?*

- Continue to draw lines to make different combinations. Call on students to use the words to make sentences with was / were going to. Encourage them to add their own endings, such as *but he changed his mind,* when appropriate.

PROCEDURE (10–15 minutes)

- Put students in groups of three, four, or five. One student mixes up the cards within each set and places them facedown in three different piles.

- Explain the activity: One player starts the timer for any amount of time between 30 and 60 seconds. He or she is the moderator in this round and does not play.

- The player to his or her left picks up one card from each pile and uses the cards to make a sentence with was / were going to. For example, if the player picks *Dave, buy an apartment,* and *affirmative statement*, then a correct sentence might be: *Dave was going to buy an apartment, but his friends talked him out of it.*

- If necessary, write some reasons for changing one's mind on the board: *I decided against it. My tastes changed. My friend talked me out of it. I changed my mind.*

- If the sentence is correct, play passes to the next player on the left. He or she takes one card from each pile and makes a sentence as explained above.

- If the sentence is incorrect, the same player tries again, using the same cards. Play does not pass to the next person until the student makes a correct sentence. The moderator is the judge of correct sentences.

- When the indicated amount of time has passed, the moderator says *Time*. The student who is making a sentence when *time* is announced gets one point. Students return all used cards to the correct piles and shuffle them.

- Note that the goal of this game is to have the least number of points, so students will try not to be the one whose turn it is when the timer goes off.

- In the next round, the new moderator is the person to the left of the previous one. He or she sets the timer and students play as described above.

- Play continues in this way until each player has been moderator twice. At the end of the game, the player with the least points wins.

OPTIONS/ALTERNATIVES (10–15 minutes)

- Students may play without the timer. They simply take turns picking three cards and using them to make a correct sentence. Students earn one point for each correct sentence they make.

- After all students have had the same number of turns (about five), the student with the most points wins.

42   ■   LESSON PLAN

Set 1

I	You	He	She	We
They	Sheri and Todd	Dave	Mr. and Mrs. Gray	Sam and Melissa

Set 2

buy an apartment	work in a dentist's office	travel to another country	start a business	have a party
go to college	have children	work with people	have the report copied	see a chiropractor
get married in Venice	hire a housecleaning service	learn another language	move to another city	get divorced
try acupuncture	study architecture	go to law school	get a picture framed	use a courier service

Set 3

affirmative statement	negative statement	question
affirmative statement	negative statement	question

Activity 22 — GROUP WORK – Role play

Unit 6 – Lesson 2

Target Language	Materials
Perfect modals	One copy of the worksheet cut into sentence strips for each group of students

PREPARATION (5 minutes)

- Say *Ken's grades weren't very good when he graduated. What should he have done?* Call on volunteers to answer the question in their own ways.

- Present the following situations and invite students to answer each question in their own ways:
  Penny loves being around people, so she became an assistant at a busy office. What other kinds of jobs would she have been good at?
  Maria didn't go to the party last night, and she didn't call. What must have happened to her?
  Mrs. Gardner has a broken arm. What might have happened?
  Gary's report didn't get to the Lima office in time for the meeting. What could he have done?

PROCEDURE (20-30 minutes)

- Put students in groups of two to five students.

- Explain the activity: Each group receives five sentence strips. Each group has ten minutes to prepare a conversation or role play for the class. The conversation may be about any topic and can include any characters. The only rule is that it must include the five sentences on the sentence strips. Students may incorporate the sentences into the conversation in any way they like.

- Encourage students to be creative, perhaps using the sentences in unexpected ways.

- Invite groups to present their conversations to the rest of the class. During the performance, students hold up the corresponding sentence strip each time they say one of the five sentences.

OPTIONS/ALTERNATIVES (15–20 minutes)

- For a quicker version of this activity, distribute only two or three sentences to each group to incorporate into a conversation. Give different combinations of sentences to each group.

- Have students vote to decide which group had the most original conversation.

You shouldn't have told everyone the truth.

I could have made a better decision.

We would have been very happy.

It might not have been hard to get there.

That must have been a big problem!

Activity 23 WHOLE CLASS – Find someone who . . .

UNIT 6 – LESSON 3

Target Language	Materials
Discussing skills, abilities, and qualifications	Half worksheet for each student, pens or pencils

PREPARATION (5 minutes)

- Write *manual dexterity* on the board and pose the following question to several students: *[Joshua], are you good with your hands?* If a student answers *yes*, ask him or her questions to get more details: *Can you tell me more about your abilities? What kinds of things do you make? What experience do you have making things?* etc.

- Repeat the exercise by asking students about *logical thinking ability* and *business experience*. Ask questions to prompt students to give more details about their skills, abilities, and qualifications.

PROCEDURE (15–20 minutes)

- Give one half of the worksheet to each student. You may choose to give all students the same half of the worksheet, or, for variety, you can give the top half to some students and the bottom half to others.

- Students review the skills, abilities, and qualifications on their worksheets. Have them fill in another skill, ability, or qualification of their choice on the blank line at the bottom of the worksheet.

- Explain the activity: Students ask one another questions about the skills, abilities, and qualifications on their worksheets. (**Note:** students should word the questions in their own way. For example, *Are you compassionate? Are you interested in science? How many languages do you speak? Are you athletic?*)

- When they find someone who has one of the skills, abilities, or qualifications, they record his or her name. Students also ask follow-up questions to learn more about the person's skill or ability. They make note of these details. For example, *What kind of experience do you have? Can you tell me more? In what ways are you artistic? What kind of sports do you play?*

- Encourage students to circulate around the classroom to talk to as many people as possible.

- After students have completed their worksheets, reconvene the class. Invite students to share information they learned by making complete sentences. For example, *Denise is artistic. She's good at drawing and painting.*

OPTIONS/ALTERNATIVES (15–20 minutes)

- If the class is large enough, instruct students not to use the same person more than once on their worksheets.

LESSON PLAN

Find someone who has . . .   **Name**   **Details**

- mathematical ability   _____   _____
- artistic talent   _____   _____
- common sense   _____   _____
- an interest in education   _____   _____
- compassion   _____   _____
- another strength:
  _____   _____   _____

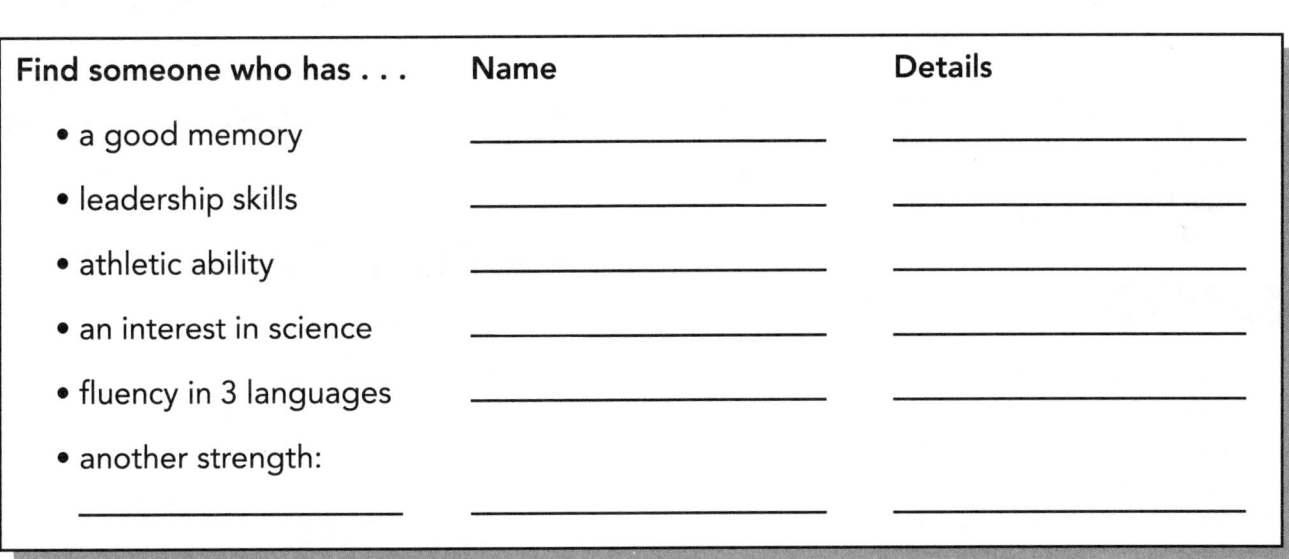

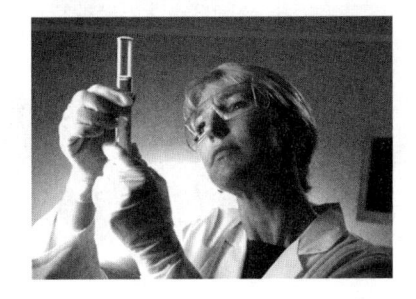

✂ -

Find someone who has . . .   **Name**   **Details**

- a good memory   _____   _____
- leadership skills   _____   _____
- athletic ability   _____   _____
- an interest in science   _____   _____
- fluency in 3 languages   _____   _____
- another strength:
  _____   _____   _____

PHOTOCOPIABLE   COPY & GO 3 ■ ACTIVITY 23   47

Activity 24   PAIR WORK – Concentration game

UNIT 6 – LESSON 4

Target Language	Materials
Discussing factors that promote success	One copy of the worksheet cut into two sets of cards for each pair of students

PREPARATION (3–5 minutes)

- Write on the board *Having some basic work habits may be effective in . . .* and then write three phrases to the right of that phrase: *prior experience; being a "complainer.";* and *promoting your success.* Read the initial phrase with the first of the three options (*Having some basic work habits may be effective in prior experience.*) Ask students, *Is this correct? (No)* Continue with the other two phrases until students decide on the correct way to finish the statement (*Having some basic work habits may be effective in promoting your success*).

- Once the correct statement has been established, agree or disagree and make a pro or a con statement. For example: *I agree. If you have routines that you follow, you will continue to do good work.* or *I disagree. If you follow the same routines, you won't stand out to those who can help promote your career.*

PROCEDURE (10–15 minutes)

- Divide students into pairs. Give each pair the two sets of cards.

- Have students shuffle each set of cards and arrange them facedown in a rectangle with three cards across and two down.

- Explain the activity: Player A turns over one card from each rectangle. If the two cards do not make a correct sentence, the player says so and turns them back over in the same spot. If the two cards make a correct sentence, the player says so and leaves both cards faceup. That player then agrees or disagrees and makes a pro or a con statement. Player B then has the opportunity to agree or disagree and make a pro or con statement and receive points. As long as students are able to make logical statements, they can keep collecting points. Students get two points for correctly matching a sentence or sentences, two points for making a logical pro or con statement, one point for correctly identifying a mismatch, and no points for incorrectly identifying a match. Then Student B takes a turn.

- When all the cards are faceup, the student with the most points wins.

OPTIONS/ALTERNATIVES (10–15 minutes)

- To speed up the game, allow students who have made a correct match to take another turn.

Answer Key

To show that you are not afraid of hard work, volunteer for assignments.

Each time you highlight a problem to your boss or management, be sure to offer solutions.

When you just talk about problems, people may think of you as a complainer.

Go out of your way to be nice to people and they will go out of their way to help you.

When you prioritize your work, you are more productive.

Remain positive in the face of all challenges.

LESSON PLAN

To show that you are not afraid of hard work,	volunteer for assignments.
Each time you highlight a problem to your boss or management,	be sure to offer solutions.
When you just talk about problems,	people may think of you as a complainer.
Go out of your way to be nice to people	and they will go out of their way to help you.
When you prioritize your work,	you are more productive.
Remain positive	in the face of all challenges.

Activity 25   GROUP WORK – Sentence-completion game

Unit 7 – Lesson 1

Target Language	Materials
Ways to commemorate a holiday; adjective clauses	Each group needs a copy of the worksheet cut into cards, a timer that measures seconds or a watch with a second hand, one sheet of blank paper per student, pens or pencils

PREPARATION (2–3 minutes)

- Write on the board the following incomplete statement:
  _____ *is a wonderful holiday for people who like chocolate.*
  Invite students to suggest possible ways to complete the sentence (*Valentine's Day, Halloween, Easter, Diwali, Day of the Dead*).

- Write another incomplete statement:
  Picnics are fun for people who _____.
  Again, invite students to complete the sentence in their own ways (*like to be outside, have children, have big families, like to eat*).

PROCEDURE (10 minutes)

- Put students in groups of four or five. One player mixes up the cards and places them facedown in a pile. He or she sets the timer for 30 to 60 seconds, chooses a card, and reads the incomplete sentence aloud.

- The player begins the timer. All players have 30 to 60 seconds to write down as many ways as they can think of to complete the sentence. For example, if the card is *Anyone who* _____ *should go to Carnaval in Rio de Janeiro,* then players might write *loves parties, likes costumes, enjoys parades, has never gone, has the chance.*

- When time is up, players take turns reading their responses aloud. If two (or more) players wrote the same response, both players cross it off their list. After all players have compared lists, players receive one point for every unique response they have. The card is set aside.

- The next player chooses another card, reads it aloud, and sets the timer. Play continues as described above. When all the cards in the pile have been used, the game is over.

- Players count up their points, and the player with the most points wins.

OPTIONS/ALTERNATIVES (10 minutes)

- Players receive one point for each correctly-formed response, whether or not it is unique.

50 ■ LESSON PLAN

Parades are fun for people who _____ .	_____ is a religious holiday that is celebrated by some people in our country.
Things that _____ make great gifts for children.	_____ is a historical holiday.
New Year's Day is a holiday that _____ .	_____ is a great holiday for people who like to eat.
Anyone who _____ should go to Carnaval in Rio de Janeiro.	_____ is a holiday that takes place in autumn.

Activity 26 GROUP WORK – Board game

UNIT 7 – LESSON 2

Target Language	Materials
Adjective clauses with subject and object relative pronouns	Each group needs one copy of the worksheet cut into cards, a game board, a die or coin for tossing, one place marker for each player (coins, poker chips, etc.)

PREPARATION (2–3 minutes)

- Write on the board the following sentences:
  A person who doesn't have a car can take the bus.
  Anyone who she wants to can enter the church.
  The band that we saw it in the parade is very good.

- Have students identify the correct sentence (the first one) and fix the errors in the other two. (*Anyone who wants to can enter the church. The band that we saw in the parade is very good.*)

PROCEDURE (15 minutes)

- Put students in groups of two or three. One player in each group mixes up the cards and places them facedown in a pile.

- Explain the game: The first player tosses the coin or rolls the die. (If using a coin, designate one side as *move one space* and the other as *move two spaces*.)

- The player moves his or her marker the indicated number of spaces. He or she reads the information on the square and plays as follows:

  - ROLL AGAIN: The player rolls the die or tosses the coin again and moves the indicated number of spaces.

  - LOSE TURN: The player's turn is finished.

  - Any other square: The player takes a card and reads the sentence aloud. He or she then states whether the sentence is correct or incorrect. If the sentence is incorrect, the player must fix it.

- If the player correctly identifies the sentence as correct, he or she stays on that square. Similarly, if the player correctly identifies the sentence as incorrect **and** is able to fix the sentence, he or she also stays on that square.

- If the player does not correctly identify a sentence as correct or incorrect, or if he or she is not able to fix an incorrect sentence, then he or she moves back to the space where he or she began.

- The next player tosses the coin or rolls the die, moves his or her marker, and plays according to the indication on the square. Play continues in this way among all players.

- The first player to reach END wins.

OPTIONS/ALTERNATIVES (10–15 minutes)

- For a simpler version of the activity, have students play without the game board. They take turns choosing a card, stating whether or not the sentence is correct, and fixing it if it is incorrect. Students earn one point for each correct answer they give. When all the cards have been used, the student with the most points wins.

- For a more challenging version, have students play in teams. Team A draws a card and reads the sentence to Team B. The sentence can be read a maximum of two times. Team B must identify the sentence as correct or incorrect, and correct the sentence, if necessary, without looking at the card. Play continues as above.

Board Game

START → Take a card. → Roll again. → Take a card. → Take a card. → Lose turn. → Take a card. → Take a card. → Take a card. → Roll again. → Take a card. → Take a card. → Take a card. → Take a card. → Lose turn. → Take a card. → Take a card. → Take a card. → Roll again. → Take a card. → Lose turn. → Take a card. → **END**

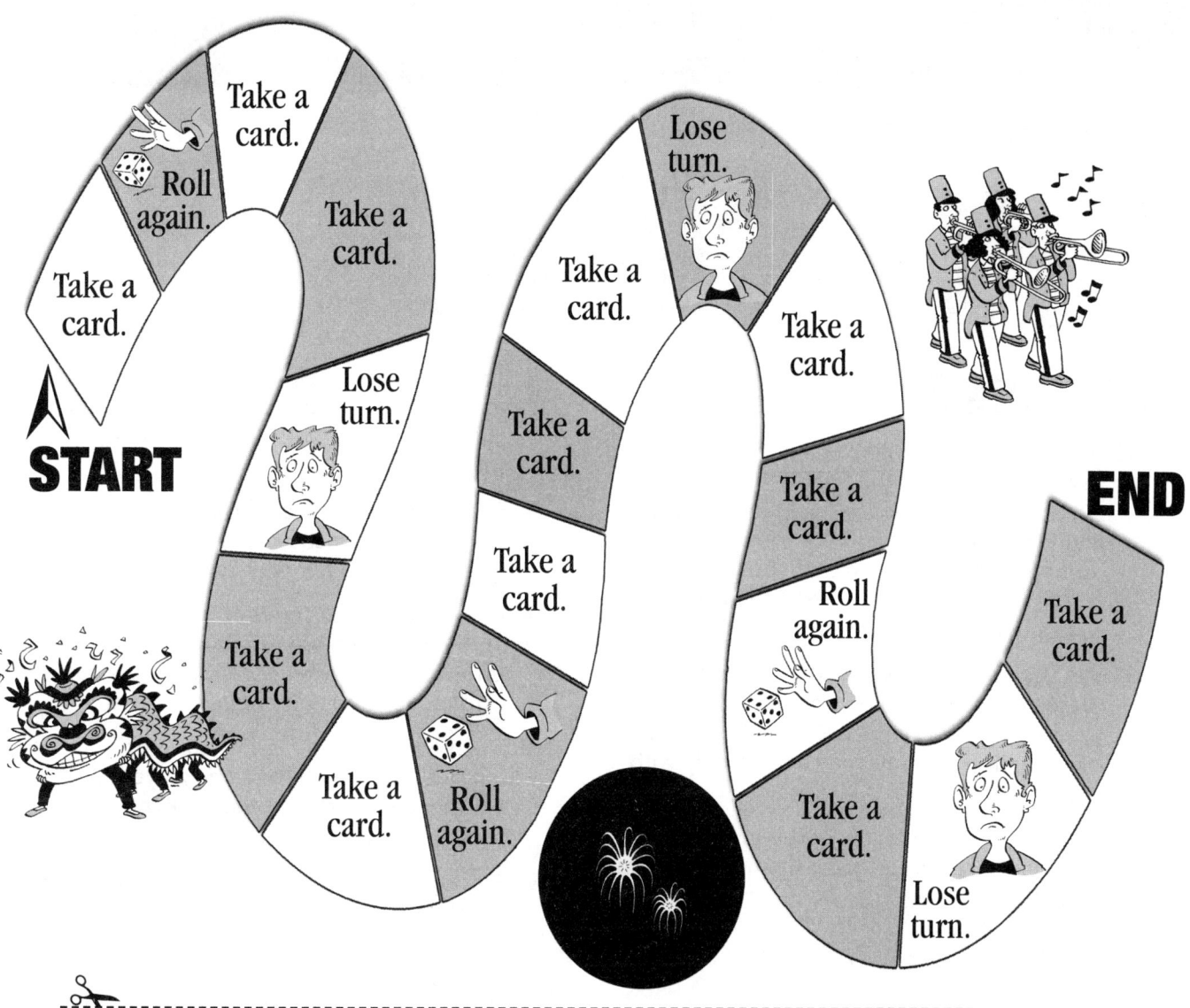

The hat he's wearing it is called a gwanmo.	Oktoberfest is a seasonal festival that began in Munich, Germany.
Boxing Day is a Canadian holiday that we celebrate on December 26.	The dance they did is called a polka.
Children's Day is a day that it honors children.	The parade that they watched it is in New York City.
A woman enters a mosque should cover her head.	In many countries a woman who she's getting married wears white.
An Indian woman who is getting married has her hands and feet decorated.	The color that it is usually associated with Valentine's Day is red.
People who travel they should learn about local customs.	A person goes into a temple should remove his or her shoes.
A person who is invited to someone's house for dinner should bring a gift.	On the Day of the Dead we remember people that they who have died.
The man I was speaking with will be at the picnic later.	The fireworks who we saw were spectacular.

PHOTOCOPIABLE

COPY & GO 3 ■ ACTIVITY 26

Activity 27   GROUP WORK – Questions game

UNIT 7 – LESSON 3

Target Language	Materials
Exchanging information about holidays	One copy of the worksheet cut into Holiday Cards and Question Cards (optional) for each group, pens or pencils

PREPARATION (2–3 minutes)

- Tell a volunteer to think of a holiday. He or she writes the name of the holiday on the board. Stand with your back to the board so other students can see what he or she has written, but you cannot. Explain that you'll ask yes / no questions about the holiday to try to guess which holiday the student is thinking of.

- Ask yes / no questions such as *Is it a historical holiday? Do people celebrate the holiday in this country? Do people eat special food on this holiday?* The students may answer only with Yes or No.

- Keep track of how many questions you ask before you're able to guess the holiday. Form your guess as a yes / no question as well, for example, *Are you thinking of Rosh Hashanah?* Tell students how many questions you asked to correctly guess the holiday.

PROCEDURE (10–15 minutes)

- Put students in groups of three, four, or five. Distribute one set of blank cards to each group. Give them 5 minutes to write one holiday on each card. Collect the completed sets of cards from all groups and redistribute each set to another group.

- One player in each group mixes up the cards and sets them facedown in a pile.

- Explain the game: One player takes a card and reads the holiday silently. The other players take turns asking yes / no questions to determine which holiday is on the card. For example, *Is it a religious holiday? Is it in the summer? Do people often give each other gifts on this holiday?*

- If students need help forming questions, you may wish to pass out copies of the optional Question Cards, which contain question suggestions.

- The player with the card can answer only Yes or No. He or she keeps track of how many questions the other players ask.

- The first player to correctly guess the holiday (in the form of a yes / no question, such as *Is the holiday Independence Day?*) takes a new card and answers other players' questions.

- If players are unable to guess the holiday within ten questions, then the same player takes another card and the others ask questions to try to guess that holiday.

- Play continues as above until there are no more cards left.

OPTIONS/ALTERNATIVES (10–15 minutes)

- You may write holidays on the blank cards before class begins. Make copies for all groups. Or you may also make just one set of cards and play the game with the whole class.

Holiday Cards

✂

_____	_____	_____
_____	_____	_____
_____	_____	_____
_____	_____	_____

Question Cards (optional)

✂

Would ____ be appropriate on this holiday?	Is it customary to ____ on this holiday?	Do people usually ____ on this holiday?
Is ____ taboo on this holiday?	Is it a religious / historical / seasonal holiday?	Do people wear costumes on this holiday?
Is it a holiday for people who ____?	Is it a holiday that takes place in ____?	Do children go to school on this holiday?
Is it common for people to ____ on this day?	Do families usually get together for this holiday?	Is the holiday ____?

PHOTOCOPIABLE

Activity 28   GROUP WORK – Trivia game

UNIT 7 – LESSON 4

Target Language	Materials
Getting married vocabulary; ways to commemorate a holiday vocabulary	One copy of the worksheet cut into cards for each group of students, pen or pencil, scrap paper for keeping score, one die for each group (optional)

PREPARATION   (3–4 minutes)

- Review the vocabulary on Student's Book pages 76 and 82. Invite students to share any facts they learned about specific holidays in this unit. (You might want to have students refer to Student's Book pages 74 and 80.)

PROCEDURE   (15–20 minutes)

- Put students in groups of four or six and then divide their group into two teams. One player mixes up the cards within each set and places them facedown in three separate piles—one-point, two-point, and three-point cards—between the two teams.

- Players on Team A decide whether they want to answer a question worth one, two, or three points. (One-point questions are the easiest, two-point questions are moderately difficult, and three-point questions are the most difficult.) A player on the other team takes a card from the corresponding pile and reads the question aloud.

- Members of Team A discuss the answer and come to a consensus. If the team answers correctly, they get the indicated number of points. Teams keep score as they play.

- Play switches to Team B and continues as above. When all cards have been read, the game is over. The team with the most points wins.

OPTIONS/ALTERNATIVES   (15–20 minutes)

- Instead of teams choosing questions by point value, they toss the die and play as follows:
  - If they roll a 1, they answer a question worth one point.
  - If they roll a 2, they answer a question worth two points.
  - If they roll a 3, they answer a question worth three points.
  - If they roll a 4, they choose the pile from which to draw a card.
  - If they roll a 5, the other team chooses the pile from which they draw a card.
  - If they roll a 6, the team loses its turn (and doesn't answer a question).

LESSON PLAN

❶ True or False: People usually eat when they have a picnic. (True.)	❷ A holiday that celebrates a certain time of the year is a ___ holiday. (seasonal)	❸ Name one of the two countries that celebrate the birthday of Simón Bolívar every year. (Venezuela, Ecuador)
❶ True or False: If two people give each other gifts, then both people receive a gift as well. (True.)	❷ Name a holiday on which people send each other cards. (Answers will vary.)	❸ In which country did mariachi bands begin? (Mexico)
❶ True or False: In some cultures it's appropriate to bring a small gift when you're invited to someone's house for dinner. (True.)	❷ What is one holiday when people watch fireworks? (Answers will vary.)	❸ In which country is the hanbok traditional clothing? (Korea)
❶ True or False: Different countries celebrate different holiday traditions. (True.)	❷ What is a woman called at the time she gets married? (a bride)	❸ What is the traditional Thanksgiving food in the United States? (turkey)
❶ True or False: If you get engaged to someone, then you agree to marry that person. (True.)	❷ What do you call a large formal party after a wedding ceremony? (a reception)	❸ During the month of Ramadan, what don't Muslims do during the day? (eat or drink)
❶ True or False: The Harvest Moon Festival is a religious holiday. (False.)	❷ What do you call a vacation taken by two people who just got married? (a honeymoon)	❸ What do you call a formal marriage ceremony? (a wedding)
❶ True or False: Some people pray on religious holidays. (True.)	❷ What is a man called at the time he gets married? (a groom)	❸ What is the name of the world-famous holiday celebrated in Rio de Janeiro, Brazil? (Carnaval)

PHOTOCOPIABLE

Activity 29   GROUP WORK – Sentence-construction game

UNIT 8 – LESSON 1

Target Language	Materials
Conditional sentences	Each group of students needs one copy of the worksheet cut into cards, one blank sheet of paper, pens or pencils

PREPARATION (2–3 minutes)

- Write the following sentences on the board:
  If it were warm and sunny today, where would you be?
  If you found a wallet on the street, what would you do?

- Invite students to answer the questions with their own information, using complete sentences.

- After students answer, ask follow-up questions to get more information. For example, if a student says *If it were warm and sunny today, I would be at the park*, you might ask *What would you do there? Who would you go with? Why would you go there?*

PROCEDURE (15 minutes)

- Put students in groups of three or four. Have them mix up the cards and spread them out faceup on a desk.

- Explain the activity: Group members work together and use the phrases on the cards to make as many present unreal conditional questions as they can. One student records each correct question as it is formed. Students can use the same words and phrases in more than one question.

- After a group has recorded at least six questions, they take turns asking and answering the questions among themselves.

- Encourage group members to ask one another follow-up questions to learn more information about their answers.

- The goal of the activity is to prompt discussion. As long as students are conducting their conversations in English, it's OK if they don't get through all of the questions or use all of the cards.

OPTIONS/ALTERNATIVES (10–15 minutes)

- After each question is read, students write their answers on strips of paper instead of saying them aloud. The strips of paper are mixed up, and students try to guess who gave each answer.

Answer Key
Answers may include, but are not limited to, the following:

If you had any job you wanted, what would you be?

If you had one wish, what would it be?

If you were an animal, what would you be?

If you were a millionaire, what would you do?

If you could travel through time, to what time would you go?

If you could go on vacation, where would you go?

If you could travel to any place in the world, where would you go?

If you could meet someone famous (alive or dead), who would it be?

If it were winter/summer/evening/2020, what would you do?

If you bought a camera/house/car, what kind would you get?

If you	one wish	any job you wanted	what would
could	travel to any place in the world	where would	you do
were	meet someone famous (alive or dead)	an animal	who would
you be	you go	it be	a car
a millionaire	go on vacation	travel through time	to what time
had	have	If it	summer
winter	evening	you	2020
get	have	you	bought
a camera	a house	what kind	would

PHOTOCOPIABLE COPY & GO 3 ■ ACTIVITY 29 59

Activity 30 GROUP WORK – Conversation

Unit 8 – Lesson 2

Target Language	Materials
Taking responsibility for a mistake; the past unreal conditional	One copy of the worksheet cut into strips for each group of students

PREPARATION (5 minutes)

- Write the following clauses on the board:
  If I had gone to the meeting, . . .
  Ellen wouldn't have gone on vacation if . . .
  If you hadn't left at 7:00, . . .

- Invite volunteers to complete the sentences in their own ways.

PROCEDURE (20–30 minutes)

- Put students in groups of two to five students.

- Explain the activity: Each group receives six text strips with sentences or clauses on them. Each group has 10 minutes to prepare a short conversation or role play for the class. The conversation may be about any topic and can include any characters. The only rule is that it must include the six sentences or clauses. Students may incorporate the sentences in any way they like.

- Encourage students to be creative, perhaps using the sentences in unexpected ways.

- Invite groups to present their conversations to the rest of the class. During the performance, students hold up the corresponding strip each time they say one of the six sentences or clauses.

OPTIONS/ALTERNATIVES (15–20 minutes)

- As a follow-up, students in the audience write past unreal conditional sentences about the conversation after each group performs. For example, *If Jack hadn't forgotten the flashlight, they would have been able to find their way home.*

- For a quicker version of this activity, distribute only two or three text strips to each group to incorporate into a conversation. Give different combinations of strips to each group.

If I hadn't done that, . . .

It wouldn't have been a problem if . . .

It was my fault.

If someone had explained the situation, . . .

Could we have done something differently?

Sorry . . .

Activity 31 — GROUP WORK – Card game

Unit 8 – Lesson 3

Target Language	Materials
Descriptive adjectives	One copy of the worksheet cut into cards for each group of students, a pen or pencil, scrap paper

PREPARATION (5 minutes)

- Put students in groups of three or four. Distribute a set of cards to each group. Give students a time limit (about three minutes) to pair cards that have the same or similar meanings. One card, the "inventor" card, will be left over.

- Review the correct answers:
  cutting-edge—state-of-the-art
  top-of-the-line—high-end
  novel—innovative
  crazy/silly—wacky
  unique—different/one-of-a-kind
  quick/fast—efficient
  slow/not working well—inefficient
  low-tech—using old methods/not modern

PROCEDURE (5 minutes)

- Students remain in their groups. One student mixes up all 17 cards and distributes them to group members. (Some students will have an extra card.) If any players have matching cards in their hand, they set them aside.

- Explain the game: The first player chooses (without looking) any card from the hand of the player to his or her left. If the player can use the card with one of his or her own to make a pair, then he or she sets aside that pair of cards. If the player can't use the card to make a match, then he or she keeps the card in his or her hand.

- Play passes to the next player to the left. He or she chooses a card from the hand of the player to his or her left.

- Play continues in this way among all players. Players continue to draw cards until all cards have been matched except for the inventor card. If a player uses all of his or her cards, then he or she is done and waits for other players to finish the game.

- The player who holds the inventor card when the last pair has been made gets one point.

- When all cards have been paired, students take turns making sentences with each pair of adjectives on their cards. For example, *My car is efficient. My stereo is state-of-the-art.*

- Players mix up all the cards and play again. After a certain number of rounds (3–5) the player with the <u>fewest</u> number of points wins.

OPTIONS/ALTERNATIVES (10–15 minutes)

- Students in each group set aside the unmatched inventor card, mix up the remaining cards, and spread them out facedown in a grid on a desk.

- One player flips over any two cards and reads them aloud.

- If the cards match, then the player picks up these two cards, sets them aside, and takes another turn.

- If the cards do not match, then the player turns the cards over again and returns them to their original positions. As much as possible, players should try to remember the location of each card as it is flipped over.

- The next player flips over any two cards. Play continues as above until all cards have been matched. The player with the most matched cards at the end of the game wins.

LESSON PLAN

cutting-edge	crazy/silly	slow / not working well
state-of-the-art	wacky	inefficient
top-of-the-line	unique	low-tech
high-end	different / one-of-a-kind	using old methods / not modern
novel	quick / fast	
innovative	efficient	

PHOTOCOPIABLE

COPY & GO 3 ■ ACTIVITY 31

Activity 32   GROUP WORK – Card game

UNIT 8 – LESSON 4

Target Language	Materials
Discussing the impact of inventions / discoveries	One copy of the worksheet cut into cards for each group of students

PREPARATION   (3–4 minutes)

- Ask students when the inventions and discoveries shown on Student's Book page 95 were invented. Allow them to refer to their books.

- Write the following years on the board:
  400 B.C.E., 711 C.E., 1256, 1489, 1738, 1834, 1902
  Have students read each year aloud. If necessary, review the meanings of B.C.E. and C.E. (B.C.E. = Before Common Era; C.E. = Common Era)

PROCEDURE   (20 minutes)

- Put students in groups of four or five. One student in each group mixes up the cards, distributes one card to each player faceup, and places the remaining cards facedown in a pile.

- Explain the game: The object is to be the first player to get five cards. Players accumulate cards by listening to an event and placing the event in the correct place chronologically in relation to the other cards he or she has.

- Play begins as follows for the first round: Player A takes a card from the pile. He or she reads the sentence, but not the date, aloud. The person to his or her left, Player B, guesses whether the event occurred before or after the date on the card Player B already has.

- If Player B guesses correctly, he or she keeps the card and places it in chronological order next to his or her faceup card to begin a timeline.

- Player B then takes a new card and reads it aloud. The person to his or her left, Player C, guesses whether the event occurred before or after the date on the card Player C already has.

- As players accumulate more cards, they must listen to the event and place it in the correct place chronologically among any other cards they have. For example, Player A reads *The first functional sewing machine was invented by a French tailor.* If Player B already has cards with events in the years 1498 and 1876, then he or she has to guess whether the sewing machine was invented before 1498, between 1498 and 1876, or after 1876.

- Any time a player guesses incorrectly, the turn passes to the next player to his or her left. This player has the opportunity to place the event in the correct place chronologically among any other cards he or she has.

- Play continues as described above. The first player to have five cards in the correct order wins.

OPTIONS/ALTERNATIVES   (5 minutes)

- After groups have finished playing, reconvene the class for a brief discussion of the inventions mentioned in the game. Invite students to say which dates surprised them. Have them discuss which of the inventions they think have been the most important.

In Brooklyn, New York, the world's first air-conditioner was used. (1902)	Wilbur and Orville Wright made the first powered flight. (1903)	The first functional sewing machine was invented by a French tailor. (1830)
The first official baseball game was played. (1846)	Alexander Graham Bell invented the telephone. (1876)	In China, Lei-yang invented paper. (about 105 C.E.)
In London, England, the world's first traffic light was used. (1868)	Coca-Cola was invented by a pharmacist, Dr. John Pemberton. (1886)	The first toothbrush was made (from bone and animal hair). (1498)
Alexander Fleming discovered penicillin. (1928)	The world's first cell phone was invented by Martin Cooper. (1973)	The world's first microwave ovens were sold. (1947)
Too busy to sit down and eat, John Montagu made the first modern sandwich. (about 1762)	Jesse W. Reno developed the first escalator. (1891)	The world's first pairs of eyeglasses were made in Italy. (about the 1270s)
Galileo Galilei invented the thermometer. (1593)	Pantyhose were invented in the United States. (1959)	Scissors were invented in Egypt. (about 1500 B.C.E.)
Peter Durand invented the tin can for preserving food. (1810)	The modern piano was developed in Italy. (about 1709)	Levi Strauss made the first blue jeans. (1873)
The Chinese began to make metal coins. (about 1000 B.C.E.)	Johann Gutenberg invented the printing press. (about 1450)	The world's first subway opened in London. (1863)
Humphry Davy, (not Thomas Edison) invented the first electric light. (1809)	The Hindu-Arabic numbering system was introduced to the West by Italian mathematician Fibonacci. (1202)	People first started to use the wheel. (3200–3500 B.C.E.)
The first public clock was made and displayed in Milan, Italy. (1335)	Dr. Edward Jenner first had the idea to use vaccinations to protect against disease. (1796)	Joseph-Nicephore Niepce was the first person to take what we now consider a photograph. (about 1827)

Activity 33 GROUP WORK – Board game

UNIT 9 – LESSON 1

Target Language	Materials
Non-count nouns that represent abstract ideas	Each group of students needs one copy of the game board, a die or coin for tossing, one place marker for each player (coins, poker chips, etc.)

PREPARATION (2–3 minutes)

- Say the following words: *advice, progress, education, politics, news, government, democracy, crime, election, information, health, time.*
- Students say whether each word is a count noun or a non-count noun.

PROCEDURE (15 minutes)

- Put students in groups of three or four.
- Explain the game: The first player tosses the coin or rolls the die. (If using a coin, designate one side as *move one space* and the other as *move two spaces*.)
- The player moves his or her marker the indicated number of spaces. He or she reads the information on the square and plays as follows:
  - ROLL AGAIN: The player rolls the die or tosses the coin again and moves the indicated number of spaces.
  - LOSE TURN: The player's turn is finished.
  - MOVE AHEAD 2 SPACES: The player moves forward two spaces and answers the question on that space.
  - MOVE BACK 2 SPACES: The player moves back two spaces and answers the question on that space.
  - Any other square: The player reads aloud the noun on the square. He or she makes a sentence with the noun. For example, if a student lands on the word *advice*, he or she might say *Allison gave me good advice when I had a problem.*

- If the sentence is correct, the player stays on that space. If the sentence is incorrect, then the player moves back to the space where he or she began.
- The next player tosses the coin or rolls the die, moves his or her marker, and plays according to the indication on the square. Play continues in this way among all players.
- Each player's sentence must be original. (Players cannot repeat a sentence that another player made on the same square.)
- The first player to reach END wins.

OPTIONS/ALTERNATIVES (15 minutes)

- A die must be used for this alternative. Each student plays with two or three place markers.
- Play as above. Each turn, players decide which of their markers they will move. Only one marker may move on each turn.
- If a player lands on a square occupied by another player's marker, and makes a correct, original sentence, he or she "takes over" the space and sends the other player's marker back to START. That player must begin anew with that marker.
- The first player to get all of his or her markers to END wins.

Board Game

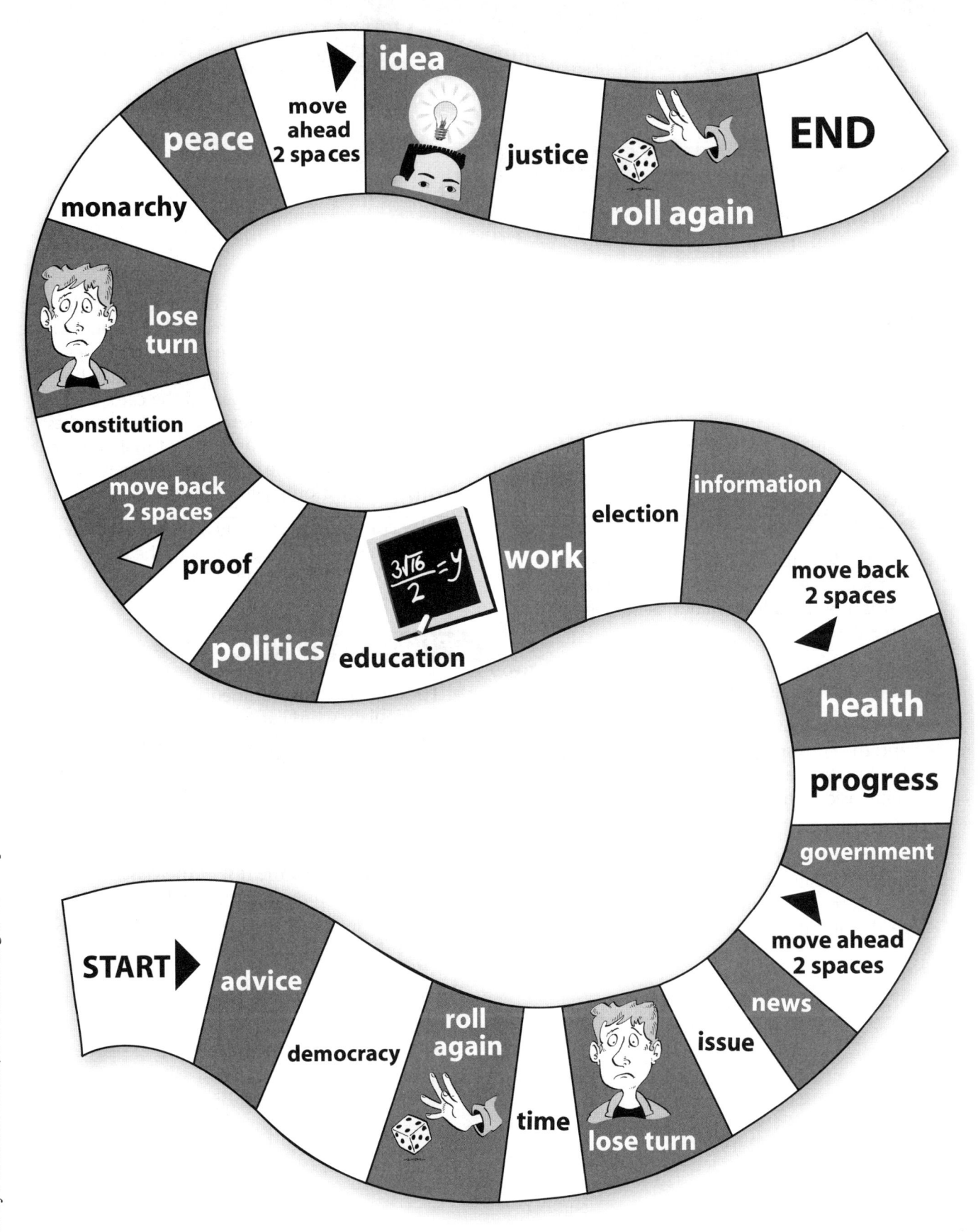

START → advice → democracy → roll again → time → lose turn → issue → news → move ahead 2 spaces → government → progress → health → move back 2 spaces → information → election → work → education → politics → proof → move back 2 spaces → constitution → lose turn → monarchy → peace → move ahead 2 spaces → idea → justice → roll again → **END**

Activity 34 PAIR WORK – Concentration

UNIT 9 – LESSON 2

Target Language	Materials
Political terminology vocabulary; political and social beliefs vocabulary; some controversial issues vocabulary	One copy of the worksheet cut into cards for each pair of students

PREPARATION (2–3 minutes)

- Read aloud definitions from the white (not gray) cards.
- Have students say the vocabulary word that corresponds to each definition.

PROCEDURE (10–15 minutes)

- Divide students into pairs (or groups of three or four). One student in each pair mixes up the cards and spreads them out facedown in a grid on a desk.
- Explain the game: One player flips over any two cards. He or she reads the cards aloud.
- If the cards match (a gray vocabulary word card and the corresponding white definition card), then the player picks up these two cards, sets them aside, and takes another turn.
- If the cards do not match, the player turns the cards over again and returns them to their original positions. As much as possible, players should try to remember the location of each card as it is flipped over.
- The next player takes his or her turn and flips over any two cards and reads them aloud. One or both cards may be the same as the ones the first player flipped over, or they may be two different cards. (Again, if the cards match, the player picks up these two cards and takes another turn. If the cards do not match, then the player turns the cards over and returns them to their original positions.)
- Play continues in this way until all cards have been matched. The player with the most cards at the end of the game wins.

OPTIONS/ALTERNATIVES (10–15 minutes)

- For this alternative, students use only the gray vocabulary word cards. Pairs or groups draw five cards and work together to create a short conversation or role play, using those words. The conversation may be about any topic and can include any characters.
- Students take turns performing their conversations for the rest of the class. During the performance, students hold up the corresponding card each time they say one of the five words.

a set of basic laws and principles that a democratic country is governed by	constitution	a government in which every citizen can vote to elect government officials	democracy
government by a ruler who has complete power	dictatorship	an occasion when people vote to choose someone for an official position	election
the group of people who govern a country or state	government	a system in which a country is ruled by a king or queen	monarchy
the art or science of government or governing	politics	to show which person you want to elect or whether you support a particular plan	vote
to succeed in (an election)	win	to be unsuccessful in (an election)	lose
supporting changes in political, social, or religious systems that respect the different beliefs, ideas, etc. of other people	liberal	having opinions or beliefs that are not extreme and that most people think are reasonable	moderate
preferring to continue to do things as they have been done in the past	conservative	supporting complete political or social change	radical
strongly opposed to political or social change	reactionary	limiting or destroying a book or film with objectionable contents	censorship
required or forced	compulsory	make less / reduce	lower
make higher / increase	raise	forbid / prevent	prohibit

PHOTOCOPIABLE COPY & GO 3 ■ ACTIVITY 34 69

Activity 35 PAIR WORK – Information-gap crossword puzzle

Unit 9 – Lesson 3

Target Language	Materials
Unit 9 social language, vocabulary, grammar	Each pair of student needs one copy of the worksheet cut in half, pencils

PREPARATION (2 minutes)

- Invite students to name some of the global problems discussed in the Student's Book.
- Encourage them to name other problems they can think of that weren't mentioned in the book.

PROCEDURE (10 minutes)

- Have students form pairs. Give each student in a pair one half of the worksheet.
- Explain the activity: Students take turns giving each other clues to complete the crossword puzzle on their worksheets. Each student has only half of the clues, so students need to work together to complete the puzzle.
- Pencils should be used, if possible, as answers may need to be erased and changed.
- If students aren't able to figure out a word based on the clue, encourage them to skip it for the moment and try it again once they have more letters filled in.
- Encourage students to compare their completed puzzles with other pairs of students to check their answers.

OPTIONS/ALTERNATIVES (2–3 minutes)

- After students have checked their answers, have them work together to write sentences, using the vocabulary from the puzzles.
- Encourage some students to read their sentences to the entire class.

Answer Key

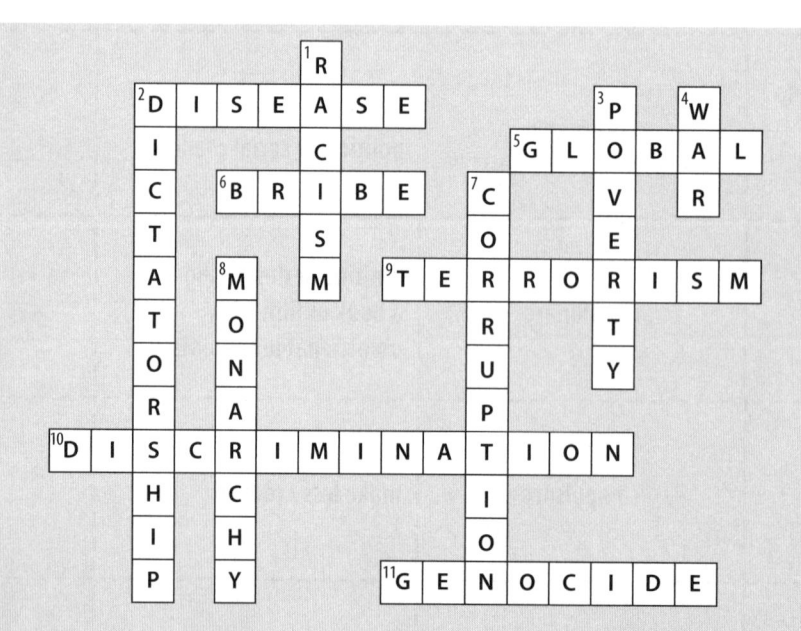

Across: 2. DISEASE, 5. GLOBAL, 6. BRIBE, 9. TERRORISM, 10. DISCRIMINATION, 11. GENOCIDE
Down: 1. RACISM, 2. DICTATORSHIP, 3. POVERTY, 4. WAR, 7. CORRUPTION, 8. MONEY

70 ■ LESSON PLAN

STUDENT A

Clues (down)

1. the belief that one's own race or ethnic group is superior to others
2. government by a ruler who has complete power
3. lack of necessary money to survive
4. violent fighting between two or more countries or between opposing groups within a country, involving large numbers of soldiers and weapons
7. dishonest, illegal, or immoral behavior, especially from someone with power
8. system in which a country is ruled by a king or queen

STUDENT B

Clues (across)

2. an illness which affects a person, animal, or plant
5. affecting or including the whole world
6. money or gift that you illegally give someone to persuade them to do something for you
9. bombings and other violent acts committed against innocent people for religious or political reasons
10. treating members of other groups unfairly
11. the attempt to destroy all members of a racial or ethnic group

Activity 36 GROUP WORK – Discussion

Unit 9 – Lesson 4

Target Language	Materials
Discussing controversial issues politely; debating the pros and cons of issues	Each student needs one set of cards (half a worksheet), pens or pencils

PREPARATION (2–3 minutes)

- Invite students to name some controversial issues. Encourage them to mention important local issues, as well as those mentioned in the Student's Book. Write the issues on the board as students name them.

- Call on volunteers to state their positions on some of the issues. Model how to form embedded questions to ask for more information. For example, *I'm curious about [why you feel that way]. I'd like to know whether [you agree with that opinion]. Could you tell me [what your reasons are for supporting that issue]?*

PROCEDURE (15 minutes)

- Put students in groups of four or five. Distribute one set of cards to each student.

- Explain the activity: The first student chooses a card. All group members find their own copy of the same card. (Cards are lettered to help identify them.) Each student completes the card however he or she likes.

- The first student collects the cards and reads the completed sentences aloud. Then students guess to whom each card belongs.

- Students ask one another to explain a little more about their feelings on each issue. Encourage them to use one or two embedded questions in their follow-up.

- The next student chooses another card. Play continues as above.

- The goal of the activity is to prompt discussion. As long as students conduct their conversations in English, it's OK if they don't get through all of the cards.

OPTIONS/ALTERNATIVES (5 minutes)

- If students have opposing viewpoints on a specific issue, they may debate the pros and cons of the issue. Remind them to use language they know to state their opinions and disagree politely.

A
I think _____ is wrong no matter what.

B
I think that _____ is morally right.

C
_____ is an important issue to me.

D
I think that _____ is the best form of government for most people.

E
I wish more people were concerned about the issue of _____ .

F
Although I'm not always in favor of _____ , I think it's OK under some circumstances.

G
I'm in favor of _____ .

H
I am a radical / liberal / moderate / conservative / reactionary. (circle one)

A
I think _____ is wrong no matter what.

B
I think that _____ is morally right.

C
_____ is an important issue to me.

D
I think that _____ is the best form of government for most people.

E
I wish more people were concerned about the issue of _____ .

F
Although I'm not always in favor of _____ , I think it's OK under some circumstances.

G
I'm in favor of _____ .

H
I am a radical / liberal / moderate / conservative / reactionary. (circle one)

Activity 37 PAIR WORK – 20 questions

UNIT 10 – LESSON 1

Target Language	Materials
Prepositions of geographical place	One worksheet for each pair, scrap paper, a pen or pencil

PREPARATION (5 minutes)

- Distribute copies of the map of Africa. Call on students to describe the location of the country of Kenya in as many ways as they can. For example, *It's on the coast. It's on the Indian Ocean. It's on the equator. It's in the central part of Africa. It's in the eastern part of Africa. It's north of Tanzania. It's east of Uganda.*

- Repeat with a few other countries if necessary.

PROCEDURE (10–15 minutes)

- Have students form pairs. Each pair needs one map. Player A secretly chooses one country on the map. He or she writes the name of the country on a piece of scrap paper and puts the paper aside.

- Explain the game: Player B asks yes / no questions about the location of the country. For example, *Is it north of Cameroon? Is it in the eastern part of Africa? Is it in the south? Is it east of the Central African Republic? Is it on a coast? Is it on the Indian Ocean?*

- Player A can answer only Yes or No. He or she keeps track of how many questions Player B asks.

- If Player B guesses the country by asking 20 questions or less, he or she gets one point. If Player B is unable to guess the country within 20 questions, then Player A gets one point.

- For the next round (regardless of who has scored), players switch roles. Player B secretly chooses a country, and Player A asks yes / no questions.

- Play continues as above. The first player to get five points wins.

OPTIONS / ALTERNATIVES (10–15 minutes)

- For a written alternative, have each student write five sentences about the map on a piece of paper. They should use blanks in place of prepositions. Collect the papers, redistribute them, and have the class fill in the prepositions in their new sentences.

PHOTOCOPIABLE

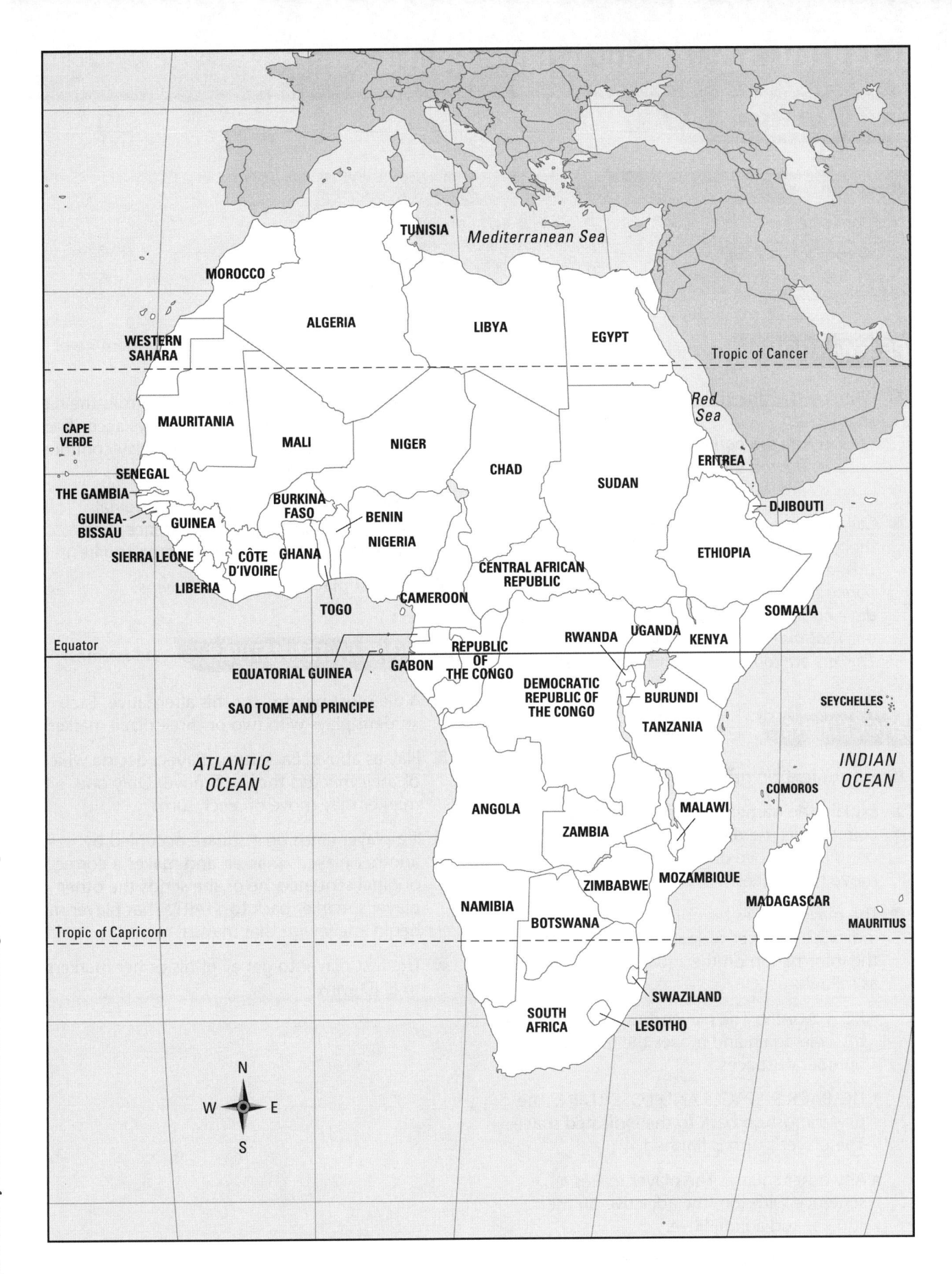

COPY & GO 3 ■ ACTIVITY 37   75

Activity 38 GROUP WORK – Board game

Unit 10 – Lesson 2

Target Language	Materials
Too + adjective and infinitive	Each group of students needs one copy of the game board, a die or coin for tossing, one place marker for each player (coins, poker chips, etc.)

PREPARATION (3–4 minutes)

- Write on the board the following incomplete sentences:
  - _____ is/are too boring to _____.
  - _____ is/are too slippery to _____.
  - _____ is/are too scary for children to _____.

- Call on volunteers to complete each sentence in their own way. For example, *Professor Johnson's classes are too boring to take. This book is too boring to read. The roads are too slippery to drive on safely. The path is too slippery to walk on. That movie is too scary for children to see. Thrillers are too scary for children to read.*

PROCEDURE (15 minutes)

- Put students in groups of three or four.

- Explain the game: The first player tosses the coin or rolls the die. (If using a coin, designate one side as move one space and the other as move two spaces.)

- The player moves his or her marker the indicated number of spaces. He or she reads the information on the square and plays as follows:

  - ROLL AGAIN: The player rolls the die or tosses the coin again and moves the indicated number of spaces.

  - GO BACK 2 SPACES AND LOSE TURN: The player must go back to the indicated space. The player's turn is finished.

  - Any other square: The player makes a sentence with <u>too</u>, the adjective on the square, and an infinitive.

- If the sentence is correct, the player stays on that space. If the sentence is incorrect, then the player moves back to the space where he or she began.

- The next player tosses the coin or rolls the die, moves his or her marker, and plays according to the indication on the square. Play continues in this way among all players.

- Each player's sentence must be original. (Students cannot repeat a sentence that another player made on the same square.)

- The first player to reach END wins.

OPTIONS/ALTERNATIVES (15 minutes)

- A die must be used for this alternative. Each student plays with two or three place markers.

- Play as above. Each turn, players decide which of their markers they will move. Only one marker may move on each turn.

- If a player lands on a square occupied by another player's marker, and makes a correct, original sentence, he or she sends the other player's marker back to START. That player must begin anew with that marker.

- The first player to get all of his or her markers to END wins.

LESSON PLAN

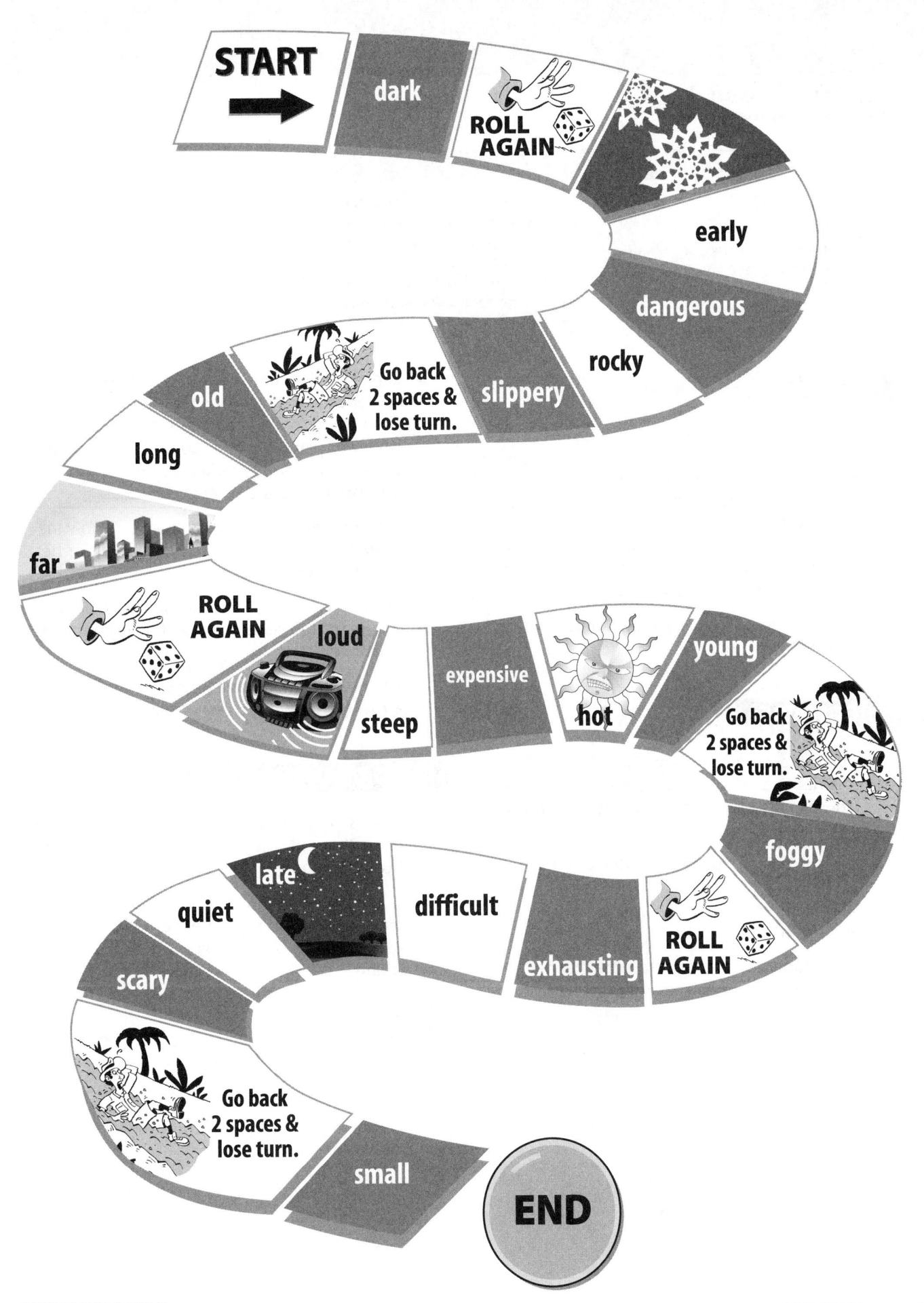

START →
dark · ROLL AGAIN · early · dangerous · rocky · slippery · Go back 2 spaces & lose turn. · old · long · far · ROLL AGAIN · loud · steep · expensive · hot · young · Go back 2 spaces & lose turn. · foggy · ROLL AGAIN · exhausting · difficult · late · quiet · scary · Go back 2 spaces & lose turn. · small · **END**

PHOTOCOPIABLE

COPY & GO 3 ■ ACTIVITY 38   77

Activity 39 GROUP WORK – Bingo game

UNIT 10 – LESSON 3

Target Language	Materials
Warning about possible risks; describing the natural world vocabulary	Each student needs one copy of the worksheet cut into picture cards, one blank piece of paper, about sixteen markers (small candies, little pieces of crumpled paper, beads, beans, etc.), glue or tape. Each group needs one set of sentence cards.

PREPARATION (5 minutes)

- Have students look at the pictures and vocabulary words on Student's Book pages 114 and 116. Make a few sentences with the vocabulary words, such as *It can be dark in the forest. It's foggy today. There are a lot of plants in the jungle. The island is surrounded by water.* Tell students to point to the picture that corresponds to each sentence.

- Invite students to make a few similar sentences of their own.

PROCEDURE (15–20 minutes)

- Put students in groups of three, four, or five. Distribute a set of picture cards to each student and one set of sentence cards to each group.

- Instruct students to glue or tape the cards to a blank piece of paper in a 4×4 grid to make a bingo board. They may place the pictures in any order they like, as long as they are in a 4×4 grid.

- One student in each group, (the "reader") mixes up the sentence cards.

- Explain the game: The reader chooses a sentence card and reads the sentence aloud. (The reader only reads in this round and does not play with a bingo board.) The other players each put a marker on the picture that corresponds to the sentence.

- For example, if the reader chooses *Follow the path*, each player puts a marker on his or her picture of a path.

- The reader chooses another sentence card and reads the sentence aloud. Play continues as above.

- The first player to have four squares covered in a row (up/down, across, or diagonally) wins.

OPTIONS / ALTERNATIVES (10–15 minutes)

- Players switch roles so that another student reads the sentences. Students exchange bingo boards and play again.

- As another alternative, students take turns picking and reading sentences. All students place markers on their bingo boards in each round.

LESSON PLAN

Be careful—it's very slippery.	It can get dark there.	There's a cave over there.	The forest is full of trees.
The steps are very steep.	This is exhausting.	The land is mountainous.	The jungle is full of wildlife.
It's foggy today.	Follow the path.	The land is hilly.	The canyon walls are tall.
This part is really rocky.	The cliff is very high.	That place is very arid.	The waterfall is breathtaking.

Activity 40 PAIR WORK – Question and answer game

Unit 10 – Lesson 4

Target Language	Materials
Describing the natural world vocabulary; discussing solutions to gobal warming	Each group of students needs one copy of the worksheet cut into cards, a coin, scrap paper for keeping score, a pen or pencil

PREPARATION (2–3 minutes)

- Ask students questions about the vocabulary on Student's Book pages 114, 116, and 118. For example, *What do you call the air, water, and land in which people, animals, and plants live? (the environment) What word means cloudy, not clear, difficult to see? (foggy) What do you call a natural hole in the earth—a cave or a cliff? (a cave) Which place probably has more plants—a canyon or a jungle? (a jungle)*
- Allow students to refer to their books if necessary.
- Encourage students to ask one another questions of their own.

PROCEDURE (10 minutes)

- Divide students into pairs (or groups of three or four). One student mixes up the cards and places them facedown in a pile.
- Explain the game: Player A tosses the coin. (Designate one side as *one point* and the other as *two points*.) This determines the number of points the player will get if he or she answers the question correctly.
- Player B takes a card and reads the question aloud. If Player A answers correctly, he or she gets the number of points corresponding to the side of the coin flipped. If Player A answers incorrectly, he or she gets zero points. Players keep score as they play.
- Students switch roles. Player B tosses the coin, and Player A reads a question.

- Anytime a *Lose a turn* card is drawn, the player's turn is immediately over and he or she gets zero points.
- Play continues as described above. The first player to get ten points wins.

OPTIONS/ALTERNATIVES (10 minutes)

- If a player answers a question correctly, he or she then has a choice. The player may take the point(s) already earned and end his or her turn. Or, the player may toss the coin again and answer another question for the opportunity to get another point(s).
- If the player answers correctly, he or she then gets the total points from both questions. However, if he or she answers incorrectly, the player gets zero points for that turn, even if he or she previously answered questions correctly in that turn. Each player keeps track of his or her own points.
- The player must decide if he or she will take another turn before tossing the coin. If he or she tosses the coin, then the player must answer a question.
- Anytime a *Lose a turn* card is drawn, the player's turn is immediately over. He or she receives no points for that turn, even if he or she previously answered questions correctly in that turn.
- On any one turn, each player must answer at least one question (unless he or she gets a *Lose a turn* card), but not more than three.
- The first player to reach ten points wins.

True or False: A jungle is usually lush. (True.)	**True or False: A jungle is usually arid.** (False.)
What word means the opposite of <u>mountainous</u>? (flat)	**What is another word that means <u>very, very tiring</u>?** (exhausting)
Name an island. (Sicily, Bali, Honshu, Grand Cayman, Hawaii, Puerto Rico, Mallorca, Taiwan, etc.)	**True or False: Mountainous land can be steep.** (True.)
Is hilly land higher than or lower than mountainous land? (lower than)	**What is the act of causing air, water, or land to become unhealthy for people, plants, and animals?** (pollution)
Which of these four words doesn't belong: <u>cliff</u>, <u>steep</u>, <u>arid</u>, <u>mountainous</u>? (arid)	**What is the word for electricity or other force that is used to make machines work?** (power)
What is a low piece of land between two mountains or hills called? (a valley)	**True or False: Energy-efficient light bulbs use more energy than older incandescent light bulbs.** (False.)
What do you call a body of land that is surrounded by water? (an island)	**True or False: Eating locally grown food is better for the environment.** (True.)
What do you call power that can be reused and never run out? (renewable energy)	**What do you call something that uses as little power as possible?** (energy-efficient)
True or False: Extremely flat land doesn't have valleys. (True.)	**True or False: Fossil fules are renewable energy.** (False.)
An area with many trees is called a _____. (forest, jungle)	**Lose a turn.**
True or False: An arid place probably doesn't get much rain. (True.)	**Lose a turn.**
Another adjective that can be used to describe beautiful scenery is _____. (breathtaking, spectacular, extraordinary, etc.)	**Lose a turn.**
What word means the opposite of <u>safe</u>? (dangerous)	**Lose a turn.**

PHOTOCOPIABLE

COPY & GO 3 ■ ACTIVITY 40

Find Someone who... and other "stand-up" activities

GENERAL TEACHING NOTES

Description

The following ten "stand-up" activities correspond to the ten units in the *Top Notch* 3 Second Edition Student's Book and are designed to be used with the units. These activities are designed to get your students to stand up and mingle in order to talk with and get specific information from each other. More than just information gathering, the goal is to practice the language learned in each *Top Notch* unit in an enjoyable and relaxed atmosphere.

In each activity, each student is given a strip of paper (the worksheet) with one or more specific tasks. In some activities, all students have the same task, and in others each student gets a unique set of tasks.

Time

Most activities can be done in about 5 to 10 minutes. In larger classes, you may want to extend the time, so students can talk to more classmates.

Materials Preparation

Before class, you will need to make enough photocopies of the worksheets for all of your students. You will need to cut them into individual strips, as shown by the dotted lines, so each student has one strip. You may wish to ask your students to help do this.

Student Preparation

Explain the goal and the specific task or tasks for each activity. Write the example questions on the board and review their structures if necessary. Explain or elicit the meanings of unfamiliar vocabulary if any.

Class Management for Larger Classes

In larger classes, you may wish to try this approach to ensure a smooth-flowing and successful activity. Divide the class in two groups. Half of the class are the questioners, the other half the respondents. The questioners mingle with the respondents and ask their questions. Then they switch roles.

Procedure

Give each student his or her worksheet. Ask students to stand up and go around the room to ask classmates their questions. Make sure students mingle and don't spend the entire time talking to only one student.

Set a time limit. When time is up, have students go back to their seats. Call volunteers to share their results with the class. Ask them what pieces of information were difficult to get or which ones they were not able to get names for.

UNIT 1 ▶ Make Small Talk

GOAL	EXAMPLE QUESTIONS	WHEN TO DO
Students try to find a person for each item on the worksheet.	How would you like to be addressed? Are you always polite?	After Lesson 4 (Student's Book page 11)

WORSHEET

Find someone who . . .   **Name**

prefers being called by his or her first name. _____

prefers being called by his or her last name. _____

prefers being addressed by a nickname. _____

prefers being addressed with a title. _____

Find someone who . . .   **Name**

has bad table manners. _____

is very punctual. _____

disagrees with the statement "When in Rome, do as the Romans do." _____

is always very polite. _____

UNIT 2 ▶ Health Matters

GOAL	EXAMPLE QUESTIONS	WHEN TO DO
Students try to find a person for each item on the worksheet.	Have you ever had a dental emergency? What happened? Do you get a yearly checkup?	After Lesson 4 (Student's Book page 23)

WORKSHEET

Find someone who . . .   **Name**   **What happened?**

- has had a dental emergency.
- has had a medical emergency.
- has used herbal medicine.
- takes vitamins regularly.
- has had an EKG.
- has had a blood test.
- has never had a shot.

Find someone who . . .   **Name**   **Why?**

- avoids X-rays.
- avoids dentists.
- doesn't get a yearly checkup.
- goes to an acupuncturist regularly.
- won't try anything but conventional medicine.
- has used homeopathy.
- takes an antihistamine.

Unit 3 ▶ Getting Things Done

GOAL	EXAMPLE QUESTIONS	WHEN TO DO
Students try to find a person who is unhappy with the businesses they use for each of the services on the worksheet.	Have you ever had a problem with a dry cleaner? Have you ever been unhappy with a car repair service? What was the problem?	After Lesson 4 (Student's Book page 35)

WORKSHEET

Find someone who has had a negative experience with a . . .	Name	What happened?
dry cleaner.	_____	_____
framing service.	_____	_____
tailor.	_____	_____
delivery service.	_____	_____
house cleaning service.	_____	_____
copy service.	_____	_____
car repair service.	_____	_____
catering service.	_____	_____
shoe repair service.	_____	_____

PHOTOCOPIABLE

UNIT 4 ▶ Reading for Pleasure

GOAL	EXAMPLE QUESTIONS	WHEN TO DO
Students get information from three other students about a book they've read or a movie they've seen.	Have you seen any good movies lately? Can you recommend a good book?	After Lesson 4 (Student's Book page 47)

WORKSHEET

Find three people who can tell you about a book they've read or a movie they've seen.

1.
Person's name: _____
Title of book or movie: _____
Who wrote or directed it? _____
What was it about? _____
Where did it take place? _____
Was it any good? _____

2.
Person's name: _____
Title of book or movie: _____
Who wrote or directed it? _____
What was it about? _____
Where did it take place? _____
Was it any good? _____

3.
Person's name: _____
Title of book or movie: _____
Who wrote or directed it? _____
What was it about? _____
Where did it take place? _____
Was it any good? _____

UNIT 5 ▸ Natural Disasters

GOAL	EXAMPLE QUESTIONS	WHEN TO DO
Students try to find someone who has heard or read about each item on the worksheet.	Have you heard or read about a flood in the last month? Where was it? What do you know about it?	After Lesson 4 (Student's Book page 59)

WORKSHEET

Find someone who has heard or read something in the last month about . . .	Name	Where?	What happened?
a flood.	_____	_____	_____
a landslide.	_____	_____	_____
a drought.	_____	_____	_____
an earthquake.	_____	_____	_____
an evacuation.	_____	_____	_____
an epidemic.	_____	_____	_____
a storm.	_____	_____	_____
a tornado.	_____	_____	_____
a hurricane.	_____	_____	_____
a power outage.	_____	_____	_____

PHOTOCOPIABLE

UNIT 6 ▶ Life Plans

GOAL	EXAMPLE QUESTIONS	WHEN TO DO
Students share information about decisions and changes in life plans.	Did you ever plan to be a teacher? Why did you change your mind?	After Lesson 4 (Student's Book page 71)

WORKSHEET

As a child, what did you think you were going to be when you grew up?

Find someone who . . .	Name	What happened?
was going to be an actor.	_____	_____
was going to be a singer.	_____	_____
was going to be a pilot.	_____	_____
was going to be a teacher.	_____	_____
was going to be a TV news anchor.	_____	_____
was going to be an athlete.	_____	_____

UNIT 7 ▶ Holidays and Traditions

GOAL	EXAMPLE QUESTIONS	WHEN TO DO
Students share information about their favorite holidays.	What is your favorite holiday? When is it? How is the holiday commemorated? What do people do?	After Lesson 4 (Student's Book page 83)

WORKSHEET

Find three people who can tell you about their favorite holiday.

1.
Person's name: _____
Type of holiday: _____
Date: _____
Why favorite? _____
Favorite customs: _____

2.
Person's name: _____
Type of holiday: _____
Date: _____
Why favorite? _____
Favorite customs: _____

3.
Person's name: _____
Type of holiday: _____
Date: _____
Why favorite? _____
Favorite customs: _____

UNIT 8 ▶ Inventions and Discoveries

GOAL	EXAMPLE QUESTIONS	WHEN TO DO
Students try to find a person who owns something that can be described by each adjective on the worksheet.	Do you own anything that is high-tech? What is it? Is it efficient?	After Lesson 4 (Student's Book page 95)

WORSHEET

Find someone who owns something that is . . .	What is it?	Who owns it?	Describe it.
high-tech.	_____	_____	_____
state-of-the-art.	_____	_____	_____
top-of-the-line.	_____	_____	_____
innovative.	_____	_____	_____
first-rate.	_____	_____	_____
wacky.	_____	_____	_____
unique.	_____	_____	_____
very efficient.	_____	_____	_____
very inefficient.	_____	_____	_____

PHOTOCOPIABLE

UNIT 9 ▶ Controversial Issues

GOAL	EXAMPLE QUESTIONS	WHEN TO DO
Students try to find a person for each item on the worksheet.	Have you heard anything in the news about censorship in the last month? Do you like arguing about politics? Why do you avoid political discussions?	After Lesson 4 (Student's Book page 107)

WORKSHEET

Find someone who has read or heard something in the news over the last month about . . .   **Name**   **What happened?**

- discrimination.
- a prohibition.
- censorship.
- corruption.
- poverty.
- an election.
- terrorism.
- hunger.
- war.
- human rights.

Find someone who . . .   **Name**   **Reason**

- hates discussing politics.
- loves discussing politics.
- tends to be a little opinionated.
- usually politely avoids political discussions.
- is optimistic about the future.
- is pessimistic about the future.

PHOTOCOPIABLE

UNIT 10 ▶ Beautiful World

GOAL	EXAMPLE QUESTIONS	WHEN TO DO
Students try to find a person for each item on the worksheet.	Have you ever been to a dangerous place? Where were you? What happened?	After Lesson 4 (Student's Book page 119)

WORKSHEET

Find someone who has . . .	Name	Where?	What happened?
been to a dangerous place.	_____	_____	_____
been on an exhausting hike.	_____	_____	_____
hiked someplace that was very steep.	_____	_____	_____
been someplace really breathtaking.	_____	_____	_____
seen a shark when he or she was swimming.	_____	_____	_____
been stung by a jellyfish.	_____	_____	_____
been to a waterfall.	_____	_____	_____
seen a volcano.	_____	_____	_____